E. J. (Edward Joseph) Lowe, W Howard

Beautiful leaved plants

E. J. (Edward Joseph) Lowe, W Howard

Beautiful leaved plants

ISBN/EAN: 9783742883520

Manufactured in Europe, USA, Canada, Australia, Japa

Cover: Foto ©Andreas Hilbeck / pixelio.de

Manufactured and distributed by brebook publishing software (www.brebook.com)

E. J. (Edward Joseph) Lowe, W Howard

Beautiful leaved plants

BEAUTIFUL LEAVED PLANTS;

BEING A DESCRIPTION OF

THE MOST BEAUTIFUL LEAVED PLANTS
IN CULTIVATION IN THIS COUNTRY;

TO WHICH IS ADDED

AN EXTENDED CATALOGUE.

BY

E. J. LOWE, ESQ., F.R.A.S., F.Z.S., F.L.S., F.G.S., F.M.S.,

Hon. Mem. Dublin Nat. Hist. Soc., Mem. Geolog. Soc., Edinb., Corr. Mem. Lyceum
Nat. Hist., New York, Corr. Mem. Manchester Lit. and Phil. Soc., Etc.
Author of a "Natural History of British and Exotic Ferns," "British Grasses," Ect., Etc.

ASSISTED BY W. HOWARD, F.H.S.

WITH SIXTY COLOURED ILLUSTRATIONS.

LONDON:
GROOMBRIDGE AND SONS, 5, PATERNOSTER ROW.
M DCCC LXVI.

TO

THOMAS BELL, ESQ.,

VICE PRESIDENT OF THE ROYAL SOCIETY,
PRESIDENT OF THE LINNÆAN SOCIETY, F.Z.S., F.G.S., COR. MEM.
PHILOMATIC AND NATURAL HISTORY SOCIETIES, PARIS,
AND OF ACAD. SCIENCES, PHILADELPHIA;
PROFESSOR OF ZOOLOGY, KING'S COLLEGE, LONDON, ETC.

My Dear Sir,

I HAVE ventured to ask permission to dedicate a Work upon "Beautiful Leaved Plants" to you, not because it merits a connection with a name so eminent in Natural History as your own, but rather as an inadequate token of respect and regard towards one who has done so much, and who still emulates the labours in the advancement of science, of your well-known predecessor at Selborne.

Believe me, My Dear Sir,

Your's Most Faithfully,

EDWARD JOSEPH LOWE.

CONTENTS.

	Plate	Page
Alocasia metallica	lx	125
Ananassa sativa variegata	xxi	43
Anœctochilus Lowii	xl	81
rubro-venia	xxxv	71
setaceus (aureus)	xxiv	49
striatus	xxx	61
xanthophyllus	vii	13
Aphelandra Leopoldii	xxvii	55
Begonia Marshallii	xviii	37
Rex	ix	17
var. grandis	vi	11
var. Isis	xii	25
var. nebulosa	xv	31
Caladium argyrites	xxii	45
bicolor splendens	iv	7
Chantini	xix	39
pictum	xliii	87
verschaffelti	xlvi	93
Calathea zebrina	i	1
Cissus discolor	xiii	27
porphyrophyllus	lix	123
Convallaria majalis variegata	xlii	85
Cordyline (Dracæna) indivisa	lii	107
Cratægus prunifolia variegata	xlviii	97
Croton pictum	viii	15
variegata	ii	3
variegatum angustifolium	xli	83
Cyanophyllum magnificum	x	21
Daphne mezereum variegatum	l	103
Dieffenbachia seguina var. maculata	xiv	29
Dioscorea discolor	liv	111
Dracæna ferrea	xxix	59
ferrea versicolor	iii	5

	Plate	Page
Echites nutans	lviii	121
Euonymus Japonicus aureus variegatus	xlix A	99
Farfugium grande	xi	23
Funkia Sieboldiana variegata	xxxiv	69
Gesnera cinnabarina	xxxiii	67
Graptophyllum pictum, or album	xlv	91
Hedera helix varieties	lvii	117
Hoya carnosa foliis-variegata	xliv	89
Hydrangea Japonica variegata	xxv	51
Maranta albo-lineata	lv	113
fasciata	xxiii	47
micans	xlix b	101
pardina	xxxii	65
porteana	xxvi	53
regalis	xx	41
vittata	xxxviii	77
Warsewiczii	xvii	35
Pandanus Javanicus variegatus	xxxvi	73
Pavetta Borbonica	v	9
Poinsettia pulcherrima	xxxi	63
Pothos argyræa	xxviii	57
Pteris argyræa	xxxvii	75
aspericaulis var. tricolor	xlvii	95
cretica var. albo-lineata	liii	109
Sonerila margaritacea	xvi	33
Tradescantia odoratissima	xxxix	79
Tussilago farfara foliis-variegata	lvi	115
Yucca filamentosa var. variegata	li	105

INTRODUCTION.

It seems necessary to say a few words with regard to a work upon plants with 'beautiful leaves,' which we purpose to give to the public in monthly parts. It is in the first place intended to bring before the public generally, a pictorial history of some of the most beautiful in this fascinating branch of horticulture. Were we to introduce to your notice all plants that had beautiful leaves, the work would necessarily become expanded into volumes, instead of what is intended, namely, a volume of the choicest and most desirable species.

It is not to a special class of plants that the attention is rivetted, but to individual plants here and there, in almost every class. The Ornamental Foliaged Plants are to be found amongst the ferns, grasses, flowering shrubs, trees, and herbaceous plants; and in many instances the leaves are so strikingly conspicuous, that the flowers amongst them only rank second in beauty. Who does not admire the *Cissus discolor, Croton variegata, Begonia rex, Calathea zebrina, Dieffenbachia picta, Dracæna nobilis, Anœctochilus argenteus, A. setaceus,* and *A. xanthophyllus,* of our metropolitan and country horticultural exhibitions? Plants are cultivated for the beauty of their leaves alone, and a hot-house well stocked with such gems will always be gay.

We are aware that all leaves are beautiful to the thoughtful and careful observer of nature; the examination of each leaf reveals beauties that to the ordinary observer would pass unnoticed. All things in nature are beautiful; it is only we who overlook or cannot appreciate or discern the loveliness of God's creations, that have their beauties hid from us.

> "Most beautiful the world is yet, and beautiful 't will prove
> Whilst one single God-made creature remains its charms to love;
> 'T is man's own sickly blindness makes the world deform'd alone;
> Who know it most, see beauty most; who know it least, see none."

But beautiful leaves, as the expression is now used, signifies something more; it means "strikingly beautiful," a plant which arrests your attention from the singularity of form, or peculiarity of colour of its leaves. It is only requisite to visit our leading Nurseries, such as Messrs. Veitch, of Chelsea; Rollisson, of Tooting; Jackson, of Kingston; Low, of Clapton; Henderson, of Pine-apple Place; and Henderson, of St. John's Wood, etc., in order to be convinced of the grandeur of these plants.

Within the last few years so many of these gems have been introduced into this country, that it is desirable that the most beautiful should be gathered together, and made the subject of a volume for the guidance of those who have only limited space for their cultivation on the one hand, and for those who would wish to have a copy of them on their drawing-room table on the other hand.

The present work needs no botanical classification; each plant figured, is strictly speaking, beautiful, and, as such, a coloured illustration and brief description has been devoted to it. Moreover it is not requisite to write a scientific description of each species enumerated, the work being intended more as a popular enumeration of such species: the book will therefore be written as popularly as possible, consistent with the accuracy of description that is deemed indispensable.

As there are very many plants that cannot find a place in this volume, it is intended to give an extended list of such species at the close of the work, that nothing may be wanting to render the history a useful addition to the library of the horticulturist.

BEAUTIFUL LEAVED PLANTS.

CALATHEA ZEBRINA.

(Maranta zebrina.)

PLATE I.

"No tree in all the grove but has its charms,
Though each its hue peculiar; paler some
And of a wannish grey; the willow such,
And poplar, that with silver lines his leaf,
And ash, far-stretching his umbrageous arm;
Of deeper green the elm; and deeper still,
Lord of the woods, the long-surviving oak.
Some glossy-leaved, and shining in the sun,
Now green, now tawny, and ere autumn yet
Has changed the woods, in scarlet honours bright."
— COWPER.

THE tribe *Calathea* in the natural order Maranths, *(Marantaceæ,)* Linnæus, 1.—*Monandria*, 1.—*Monogynia*, are stove herbaceous perennials.

The name is from the Greek *Kalathos* signifying *a basket*, on account of the leaves being worked into baskets in South America.

Calathea zebrina, the Zebra Calathea, is a native of Brazil, the plant having been introduced into this country in 1815.

Summer temperature 65° to 75°, winter temperature 55° to 60°.

A well-known plant in our stoves, yet when successfully grown inferior to none for fine foliage.

An evergreen herbaceous plant, with leaves two feet long and six inches wide. Each leaf is beautifully barred with greenish purple, and has a soft appearance, resembling the finest velvet.

The flowers, which spring from the root in a spike-like form, are of a rich purple colour, shaded with red and white.

Easily propagated by division of the root, the plant producing side-shoots, which should be cut off from the main plant without injury to the roots belonging to each division. Shade these plants for a month from the sun's rays, after which they may be treated like established plants.

The best compost is a moderately rich soil, consisting of fibry loam and sandy peat in equal parts, with about an eighth of well-decomposed cow dung and vegetable mould.

Give the plants larger pots every spring, watering abundantly during the summer months, and more moderately in winter. The plants will grow much more luxuriantly if plunged in bottom-heat. Plants so grown will have leaves three feet long, each plant covering a space three feet in diameter, and will excite universal admiration.

The illustration is from a plant from the collection of Mr. Howard, of Dykes Hall, near Sheffield.

CROTON VARIEGATA.

CROTON VARIEGATA.

PLATE II.

"Gorgeous flowerets in the sunlight shining,
  Blossoms flaunting in the eye of day,
Tremulous leaves, with soft and silver lining,
  Buds that open only to decay.

Wondrous truths, and manifold as wondrous,
  God hath written in those stars above;
But not less in the bright flowerets under us
  Stands the revelation of His love."

LONGFELLOW.

THE tribe *Croton*, in the natural order Spurgeworts, (*Euphorbiaceæ*,) Linnæus, 21.—*Monœcia*, 10.—*Monadelphia*, are allied to *Jatropha*, from the roots of which tapioca is made.

Croton is derived from the Greek *Kroton*, signifying *a tick*, in allusion to the shape of the seeds.

The *Crotons* are nearly all stove evergreen shrubs. Croton oil, the most powerful of purgatives, is obtained from the seeds of *Croton tiglium*.

Croton variegata, the Variegated-leaved Croton, was introduced into this country in the year 1804. It is a native of the East Indies.

A stove evergreen shrub, growing from eight to ten feet high.

Summer temperature 65° to 75°, and winter temperature 55° to 60° Fahrenheit.

Readily increased by cuttings taken off in March or April. The cutting-pot should be well drained, placing upon the drainage a thin layer of moss, above which a light compost of loam and sandy peat in equal parts, and above this an inch of pure silver sand. Gently water to make the sand firm, and then put in the cuttings. Place a bell-glass over the pot, and use clean sticks to keep the leaves from touching the glass. With a very sharp knife smooth the base of the cutting, and preserve the top leaves entire. Plunge the pot in bottom-heat and shade it from the sun. In six weeks the cuttings will be sufficiently rooted to pot off; after this is done shade them again until they are established. Every spring add leaf mould to the compost, but do not overpot. Water moderately, especially in winter.

The habit of the plant is somewhat straggling, therefore to form a handsome low bush it is necessary to stop the leading annually, and to train out the side branches.

The leaves are about six inches long, and one inch and a half wide in the centre. They are very handsome, being densely variegated, striped, and mottled with yellow on a green ground.

There is no variegated plant that surpasses this in beauty when well grown and fully exposed to bring out the bright colours. The flowers are white and green.

It is worthy of being grown in every stove, however small.

The illustration is from a plant in the collection of Mr. James Hodge, Wadsly House, near Sheffield.

DRACÆNA FERREA VERSICOLOR.

(Terminalis.)

PLATE III.

"It seems a foolish fancy, yet 't is mine
 That flowers now peeping on the doubtful skies,
Do by their beauty ask the sun to shine,
 Therefore he kisses then their golden eyes.

> And in his love arrays them in all hues,
>   That live dissolved in his essential beams;
> And on them airy perfumes doth diffuse,
>   As such bright things of beauty best beseems.
>
> 'T is thus the beautiful of woman born,
>   In speechless asking and unbreath'd desire,
> Turn to the sun of love's unclouded morn,
>   And catch their brightest tinges from its fire."
>
> HOOTON.

Dracæna is derived from the Greek *Drakaina*, meaning a *female dragon*, because the milky juice from the Dragon Tree on drying becomes a gum, having the same properties as the resinous substance known as dragon's blood.

Natural order Lilyworts, *(Liliaceæ,)* Linnæus, 6.—*Hexandria*, 1.—*Monogynia*.

Stove or greenhouse evergreens, above a score species of which are known in this country.

Dracæna ferrea versicolor, or the Various-coloured Terminal Dragon Tree.

Native of the East Indies. Introduced into this country in 1820.

A stove evergreen, growing ten or fifteen feet high.

This beautiful foliaged plant requires the heat of the stove. Summer temperature 70° to 80°, winter temperature 50° to 60°.

Propagation. When several plants are required, cut down an old plant and divide the stem into lengths an inch long, plant these overhead in a pot of light sandy earth, and plunge into brisk bottom-heat, when every piece will quickly become a plant. The top may also be struck in sand, under a bell-glass. By planting large pieces of the stem overhead in a warm tan-bed, good plants may be produced in one year.

The cuttings should be potted off as soon as rooted, in a compost consisting of loam, peat, and leaf mould, and shaded for a few days.

This plant is inclined to run up with one stem, to prevent which let the leading shoot be cut out.

The leaves are nearly a foot long, and from two to three inches wide. They are of a dark cinnamon colour, richly shaded with brilliant scarlet and crimson of various shades.

A somewhat common plant, but nevertheless exceedingly handsome.

The illustration is from a plant in Mr. Howard's collection.

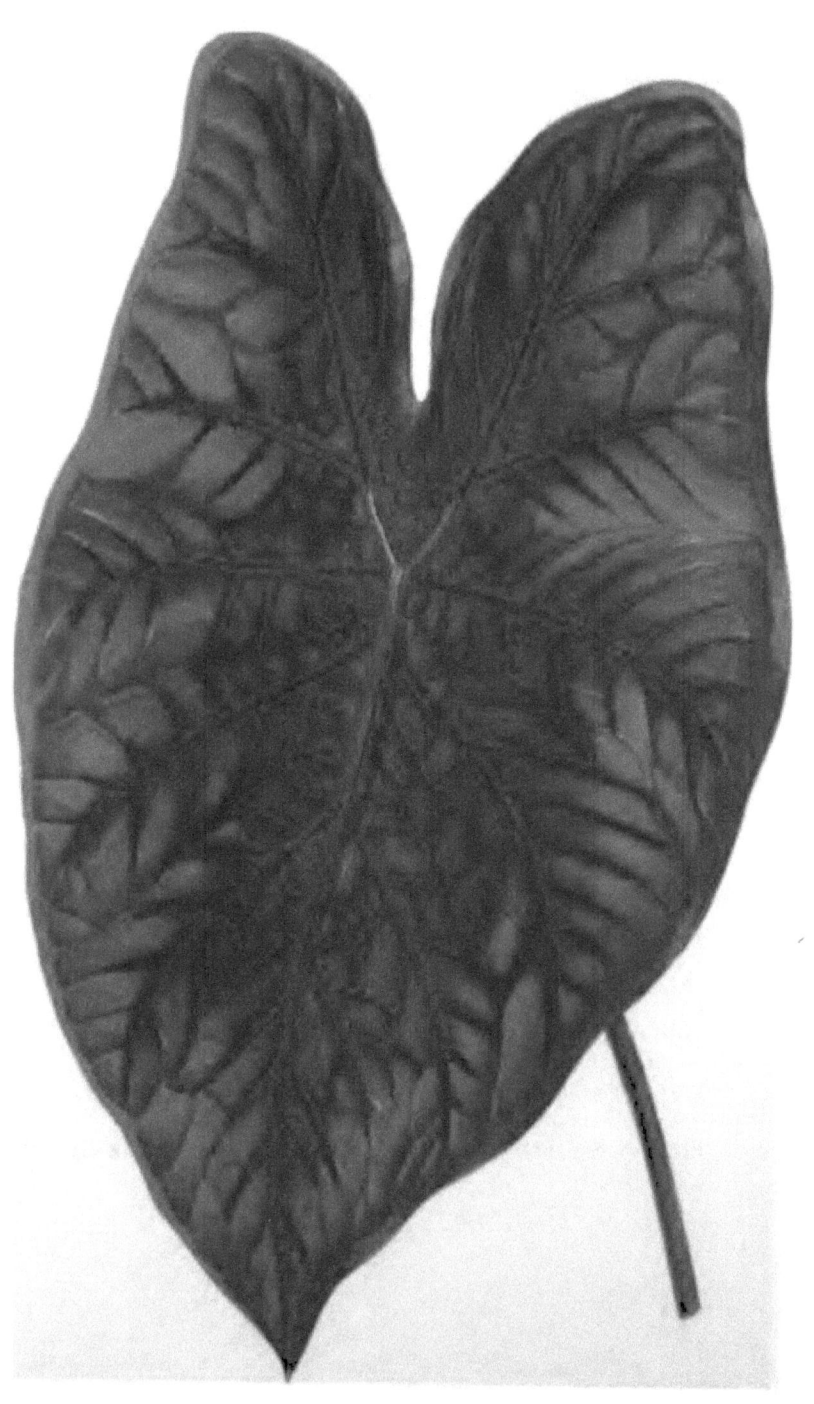

CALADIUM BICOLOR SPLENDENS
IV

CALADIUM BICOLOR SPLENDENS.

PLATE IV.

> "Who loves a garden loves a greenhouse too.
> Unconscious of a less propitious clime,
> There blooms exotic beauty, warm and snug,
> While the winds whistle, and the snows descend.
> The spiry myrtle, with unwithering leaf,
> Shines there and flourishes. The golden boast
> Of Portugal and Western India there,
> The ruddier orange, and the paler lime,
> Peep through their polish'd foliage at the storm,
> And seem to smile at what they need not fear."
> COWPER.

Caladium, in the natural order Arads, *(Araceæ,)* Linnæus, 21.—*Monœcia,* 9.—*Polyandria,* is allied to the genus *Colocasia.*

The ginger-like roots of *Caladium bicolor* are used as food in tropical countries, under the name of cocoa roots.

Stove evergreens or stove herbaceous plants, with the exception of *Caladium Virginicum*, which comes from Virginia, and is quite hardy in this climate.

There is an interest attached to these plants on account of the beauty of their stems and leaves.

Caladium bicolor splendens, the Splendid Two-coloured Caladium, is a native of Madeira, having been introduced into this country as early as 1773. It is a deciduous stove herbaceous plant, the foliage dying down in the autumn.

Summer temperature 70° to 80°, winter temperature 55° to 60°. The plant attains the height of two feet.

The leaves when well grown are truly magnificent; they are about nine inches long, and seven inches broad. The centre of each leaf is of a glossy metallic lustre, between scarlet and crimson; the margin of each leaf being dark green.

Flowers white.

Increased by division, and by small bulbs or tubers.

The plants which lie dormant in winter should in spring have all the old soil shaken from them. Pot in a compost consisting of peat, turfy loam, and well decomposed cow dung. Drain the pots well, and plant the tubers about half an inch deep; give bottom-heat, but no water until the leaves begin to appear, then gradually increase the quantity as the plant advances in growth. In October allow the plants gradually to dry off, and then put them on a shelf, out of the way of moisture and frost.

For plants we are indebted to Mr. Lamb, gardener to Mr. F. Wright, of Osmaston; Mr. Jackson, Nurseryman, Kingston; and to Mr. Rollisson, of Tooting.

The illustration is from a plant in the collection of Mr. Howard.

PAVETTA BORBONICA.

PLATE V.

> "Within the garden's peaceful scene
> Appear'd two lovely foes,
> Aspiring to the rank of queen,
> The lily and the rose."
>
> — Cowper.

The genus *Paretta* is allied to *Ixora*, Linnæus, 4.—*Tetrandia*, 1.—*Monogynia*, natural order Cinchonads, *(Cinchonaceæ.)* The various species are natives of China, the Cape of Good Hope, and the East Indies, and the present species, introduced about the year 1810, from the Isle of Bourbon, hence its specific name.

A stove species. Summer temperature 70° to 80°, winter temperature 50° to 60°.

Rare in cultivation; flowers not showy. The habit of the plant is good, but requiring stopping in order to form a bushy object. The leaves, which are magnolia-like, are about nine inches long, beautifully spotted with concentric rings of white, shaded with pale green on a dark green ground, the mid-vein of the leaf being salmon red.

Propagation. Cuttings taken off early in March, before the plant begins to grow, and placed in sand under a tall bell-glass, the leaves being propped up with clean sticks, in order to prevent them touching the sides of the glass. Plunge in a brisk bottom-heat, and they will readily strike root. Carefully shade with a sheet of white paper. Pot off as soon as rooted, and continue the shading for a few days, in order to allow the plants time to establish themselves.

Culture. Re-pot when the first pots are filled with roots, using the following compost:—Fibry loam and sandy peat in equal parts, using no stimulating manures. Give the plant plenty of light and air, in order to produce a stout growth, and to bring out the beautiful tints on the leaves.

The illustration is from a plant in the collection of Mr. John James, Washington Road, Sheffield.

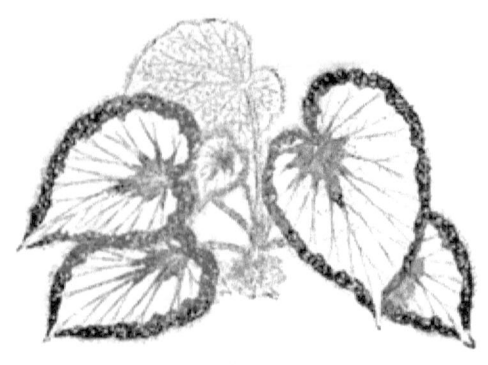

BEGONIA REX.—Variety Grandis.

ROLLISSON.

PLATE VI.

"So, farewell, great forest teachers,
There is a spirit dwells
In the veinings of each leaflet,
In each flower's cells.
Ye have each a voice and lesson,
And ye seem to say—
'Open, man, thine eyes to see
In each flower, stone, and tree,
Something pure and something holy,
As thou passest on thy way.'"
F. C. W.

RAISED from seed in 1858, by Messrs. Rollisson and Sons, of Tooting.

An herbaceous stove plant, a foot high, and of a spreading habit. The leaves are eight inches long and six inches wide, and of an oblong-oblique heart-shaped form. Colour brownish olive green, with an irregular zone of white, which shews through the leaf. The stem and leaf covered with scarlet hairs, the ends tipped with white; on the under side the leaves are a rich crimson. Flowers large, and of a pink colour.

The present magnificent variety, with several others equally beautiful, have been raised from *Begonia rex*. As none of them can be passed over in silence, we shall return to the subject in a future number.

CULTURE.

This hybrid requires a warm moist stove all the year; summer temperature 75° to 80°, winter temperature 65° to 70°.

Soil, fibry loam one part, sandy fibry peat two parts, leaf mould one part, well mixed with silver sand. Re-pot in March, and give abundance of water in summer, but more moderate in quantity in winter; drain the pots securely.

Propagation. Take a leaf and cut it into several pieces, plant thickly in a pot well drained and filled to within an inch of the top with the compost, and the remaining inch with pure silver sand; give a gentle watering, and place the pot under a shaded bell-glass, in a moist bottom-heat. A bed of sand is the best. At the base of each leaf roots and young small leaves will speedily appear. As soon as the young leaves are formed take them up, put into small pots, and replace them in bottom-heat till a fresh growth is perceived, then gradually inure them to bear full light.

The seedlings referred to above are really a boon to the lovers of beautiful foliaged plants, indeed, whoever wishes to have a treat should visit the Messrs. Rollisson's Nursery, and inquire for the *Begonia* house. They have devoted an entire house to their culture, and it is truly splendid with the rich colours of these new and interesting plants.

The illustration is from a plant of the Messrs. Rollisson and Sons, of Tooting, near London.

ANŒCTOCHILUS XANTHOPHYLLUS.
VII

ANŒCTOCHILUS XANTHOPHYLLUS.

PLATE VII.

"Flowers as the changing seasons roll along,
Still wait on earth, and added beauties lend.
Around the smiling Spring a lovely throng
With eager rivalry her steps attend;
Others with Summer's brighter glories blend;
Some grace mild Autumn's more majestic mien;
While some few lingering blooms the brow befriend
Of hoary Winter, and with grace serene
Enwreath the king of storms with mercy's gentle sheen."

Bernard Barton.

A MAGNIFICENT genus of stove evergreens from Java, India, and Ceylon, growing in the hedgerows. The name is derived from two Greek words, *Onoikios*—open, and *cheilos*—a lip, in reference to the spreading apex of the lip. Linnæus, 20.—*Gynandria*, 1.—*Monandria*. Natural order Orchids, (*Orchidaceæ.*)

The natives of Ceylon call the *Anœctochilus setaceus* the "King of the Woods," not from the flowers, which are insignificant, but from the leaves, which are the most beautiful among plants. The different varieties have rich velvety leaves, having a metallic lustre, and being curiously inlaid with streaks of golden and frosted net-work, some of the species having in addition a broad golden band down the centre of each leaf.

Anœctochilus xanthophyllus was introduced by Messrs. Veitch, of Exeter, in 1849, from Java.

A low creeping plant, with curious, although not showy flowers, the leaves being the feature of attraction; nothing can exceed their loveliness. The leaves are not large, seldom exceeding from two to three inches in length, and an inch in breadth. The ground-colour of a rich dark velvety appearance, of a shining metallic lustre. The veins are golden, and a broad stripe of yellow spotted with brown extends on each side of the midrib. No description, however, can do justice to the beauty of these leaves; even our artist, with all his skill, cannot transmit to paper the glowing metallic lustre visible on these apparently inlaid-with-gold leaves.

Summer temperature from 70° to 90°, winter temperature from 60° to 70°.

Propagation. Increased by division; each piece so divided should have roots to insure its growth.

Culture. Pot in very sandy rough peat, mixed with chopped sphagnum and a few pieces of charcoal; the pots to be well drained, and the plants constantly covered with bell-glasses and kept in a shady part of the stove. Great care is requisite in watering; the leaves must never be wetted, and in winter the soil should be kept only just damp. The glasses require wiping every day, or the leaves will damp off.

The illustration is from a plant in Mr. Howard's collection.

CROTON PICTUM.

PLATE VIII.

"I would sing of you, sweet wild-flowers, in the far-sequestered glade,
Where noble pines and ancient oaks cause deep and solemn shade;
Where tufts of early primroses, and hidden violets grow,
While list'ning to the wooing of the murm'ring brook below;
Where the heather and the harebell grace the red deer's fairy home,
And the feathery ferns in beauty wave beneath the azure dome;
And where, roaming o'er the purple hills, I tread the dewy sod,
And muse on Nature's splendour, in communion with her God."

We have given a description of the genus *Croton* in describing *Croton variegatum*.

The present species was introduced from the East Indies in the year 1810.

A stove evergreen. Summer temperature 65° to 75°, winter temperature 55° to 60°.

Habit rather straggling. In order to produce a handsome specimen stop the leading shoots annually, and train out the side-shoots.

The leaves are about six inches long, and two inches wide in the centre. They are very handsome, being shaded and spotted with crimson and red in curious patches. It is not uncommon in good collections, and is worthy of being in every stove, however small.

Propagation. Readily increased by cuttings taken off in March and April, and planted in a prepared cutting-pot. Drain well by first placing a large piece of broken pot over the hole at the bottom, then a layer of small pieces, and over this a layer of still smaller pieces, and upon which a thin layer of moss, then fill the pot to within an inch of the rim with a light compost, consisting of equal parts of loam and sandy peat, upon which place an inch of pure white sand. Give a gentle watering, and fit on a bell-glass within the rim of the pot.

Take off the cuttings, preserving the top leaves entire, and with a very sharp knife smooth the base of each cutting. Plant in the centre of the pot, and prop up the leaves with clean sticks to prevent them from touching the glass. Give a gentle watering to settle the sand close to the cuttings, and after allowing the leaves to dry, fit on the bell-glass, and plunge in bottom-heat, shading from the sun. In six weeks roots will be emitted, and the plants should be potted, taking care to shade until established.

Culture. Every spring add some leaf-mould to the compost. Be careful not to over-pot; at first water moderately, especially in winter.

The illustration is from a plant in Mr. Howard's collection.

BEGONIA REX.
IX

BEGONIA REX.

PLATE IX.

"Beautiful children of the woods and fields!
That bloom by mountain streamlets 'mid the heather,
Or into clusters, 'neath the hazels, gather,—
Or where by hoary rocks you make your bields,
And sweetly flourish on through summer weather—
                    I love ye all!

Beautiful things ye are, where'er ye grow!
The wild red rose—the speedwell's peeping eyes—
Our own blue-bell—the daisy, that doth rise
Wherever sunbeams fall or winds do blow,
And thousands more, of blessed forms and dies—
                    I love ye all!

Beautiful objects of the wild bee's love!
The wild-bird joys your opening bloom to see,
And in your native woods and wilds to be,
All hearts, to nature true, ye strangely move,
Ye are so passing fair—so passing free—
                    I love ye all!

Beautiful children of the glen and dell—
The dingle deep—the moorland stretching wide,
And of the mossy fountain's sedgy side!
Ye o'er my head have thrown a lovesome spell,
And, though the Worldling, scorning, may deride—
                    I love ye all!"
                  Robert Nicholl.

BEGONIA is named after M. Begon, a French patron of botany.

A numerous genus of stove evergreen shrubs, herbaceous perennials, or tuberous-rooted plants. Native of Jamaica, Brazil, the West Indies, East Indies, Guatemala, Mexico, Peru, Cape of Good Hope, South America, Nepaul, etc. Varying in height from six to sixty inches.

A most lovely tribe of plants, beautiful both for their leaves and flowers.

Begonia rex is a native of South America.

It was introduced into this country in the year 1857, by Messrs. Rollisson, of Tooting, who received it from M. Linden, a nurseryman at Berlin.

B. rex is the most magnificent of the species, and will give place only to seedling varieties raised from it last year by Messrs. Rollisson, of Tooting. Amongst them there are some of the finest variegated-foliaged plants that it would be possible to conceive, and the cultivator of this class of plants will hail these additions with gratification.

An evergreen herbaceous stove plant, requiring a moist atmosphere.

Summer temperature from 70° to 80°, winter temperature from 60° to 65°.

The leaves are large, of an oblique-oval shape. Ground-colour of the leaf a dark green, having a broad band of pure white about mid-way between the margin and the centre. Petioles reddish green, covered with short hairs. Stem short.

Flowers pretty but not showy, and of a pale yellowish white on the upper surface, and light brown underneath.

Culture. Soil, a light rich compost of sandy turfy loam, sandy fibrous peat, and decayed leaves in equal parts. The plants should be rather under-potted, as when in too large pots the variegation is not so clear.

Propagated by the leaf. Take a moderate-sized leaf, lay it flat on the surface of a pot filled with sand, cut the ribs into several divisions, and peg the leaf down with small hooked sticks, place the pot on a heated surface and cover with a hand-glass. Shade from the sun, and keep the internal air moderately moist. In a very short time roots will be produced at the base of each division, and young leaves will appear, gradually forming a new plant, which may then be carefully taken up and potted, and replaced for a short time in a close moist heat until fresh growth is perceived, after which gradually inure them to bear the full light and air. Re-pot frequently. In six months the plants so treated will be a foot across, bearing numerous large splendid leaves.

Our thanks are due to Messrs. Rollisson, of Tooting, for a plant of this species.

Amongst the hundreds of seedlings raised from *Begonia rex* by Messrs. Rollisson and Son, six, namely, *grandis*, *urania*, *nebulosa*, *virginia*, *rollissonii*, and *isis* are very distinct and beautiful. The variety *grandis* has been already figured on Plate VI. of this work, and the others will again be referred to and several of them figured.

The wood-cut illustration is from a photograph of a plant in the collection at Highfield House.

CYANOPHYLLUM MAGNIFICUM.

X

CYANOPHYLLUM MAGNIFICUM.

PLATE X.

"By fetters forged in the green sunny bowers,
As they were captives to the King of Flowers."
                                            Moore.

NATIVE country Tropical America. Introduced in 1857, by M. Linden, a continental Nurseryman.

A fine woody melastomaceæ stove shrub, which has not yet flowered in this country. The leaves are truly magnificent, growing two feet long and nine inches wide; of a long oval shape, tapering to a point. Upper surface a distinct ivory-like midrib, with a pair of veins of the same colour running from the base near the margin and meeting near the point, joining there the midrib. Margin irregularly serrated. Colour a deep velvety green; underneath the veins are visible, and the general colour is a rich purplish crimson. Habit strong-growing.

Nothing can possibly exceed the beautiful foliage of this truly handsome new plant. The flowers are said to be very beautiful also, but fugacious.

Culture. Heat required 70° to 75° in summer, 65° to 70° in winter. Soil equal parts of peat and vegetable mould, with a good sprinkling of silver-sand, well incorporated together. Pot in spring, draining well; water freely during the warmer months, and expose the plant fully to the sun to bring out the colours; in winter water sparingly. The syringe may be used in the evening when the plant is growing freely. It has a tendency to run up with a single stem; if a bushy plant is desired the top may be taken off, and again from the side shoots when they have made a little progress.

Propagated by cuttings, which should be inserted in sand in pots placed under a handlight on a heated surface, and shaded from the sun; the leaves should be kept entire, and propped up with small clean white sticks. It is not difficult to increase in this way.

The engraving is from a plant in Mr. Howard's collection; and the coloured plate from a plant of the Messrs. Rollisson, of Tooting.

FARFUGIUM GRANDE
XI

FARFUGIUM GRANDE.

PLATE XI.

> "How beautiful! A garden fair as heaven,
> Flowers of all hues, and smiling in the sun,
> Where all was waste and wilderness before.
> Well do ye imitate, ye gods of earth,
> The great Creator."
>
> GOETHE.

A VERY interesting new plant. Native country North China. Sent home to Mr. Glendinning, of the Chiswick Nursery, by Mr. Robert Fortune, in the year 1855.

A greenhouse evergreen plant, with heart-shaped rounded leaves, beautifully blotched and spotted thickly with yellow on a dark green ground. Leaf-stems one foot long; leaves nine to twelve inches in diameter.

An almost hardy plant, as it will stand the winter in the

south, but loses its foliage. In a collection of variegated plants it is a conspicuous object, the spots are so distinct and striking. The plant forms a dense bush from three to four feet across, and two feet high.

Culture. Strong fibry loam, sandy peat, and decomposed vegetable mould, mixed in equal parts, will grow this plant well. Pot rather freely twice a year, the first time in March and the second in August. The variegation is improved by full exposure near to the glass of a good greenhouse or in a cold frame.

Propagation. The plant sends up side suckers, which may be taken off with roots, potted, and placed under a handlight or cold frame until new roots are formed. Then repotted, and placed in a cold frame, shaded for a few days, after which they may be hardened off and placed on a shelf near the glass in the greenhouse.

I am indebted to Mr. Cooling, of Derby, for a plant of *Farfugium grande*.

BEGONIA REX.—Var. Isis.

Rollisson.

PLATE XII.

> "And what a wilderness of flowers!
> It seem'd as though from all the bowers
> And fairest fields of all the year,
> The mingled soil were scattered here.
> The lake, too, like a garden breathes,
> With the rich buds that o'er it lie,—
> As if a shower of fairy wreaths
> Had fall'n upon it from the sky."
>
> Moore.

An exceedingly beautiful hybrid, raised at Tooting Nursery from *Begonia Rex*, in the year 1858, and sent out on the 1st. of May, 1859.

The leaves, which are without spots or hairs, are of a rich metallic silvery hue, having a border of an olive green, which latter is slightly covered with hairs. Near the stem the leaf is green. The stem is red and hairy.

Easily cultivated and propagated as mentioned with *B. Rex*, and *B. Rex* variety *grandis*, (see Plates VI. and IX., and pages 11 and 18.)

As it would be unnecessary to repeat what has been said in describing *B. Rex* and its variety *grandis*, the reader is referred to them.

For a specimen of this beautiful plant my thanks are due to Messrs. Rollisson, of Tooting.

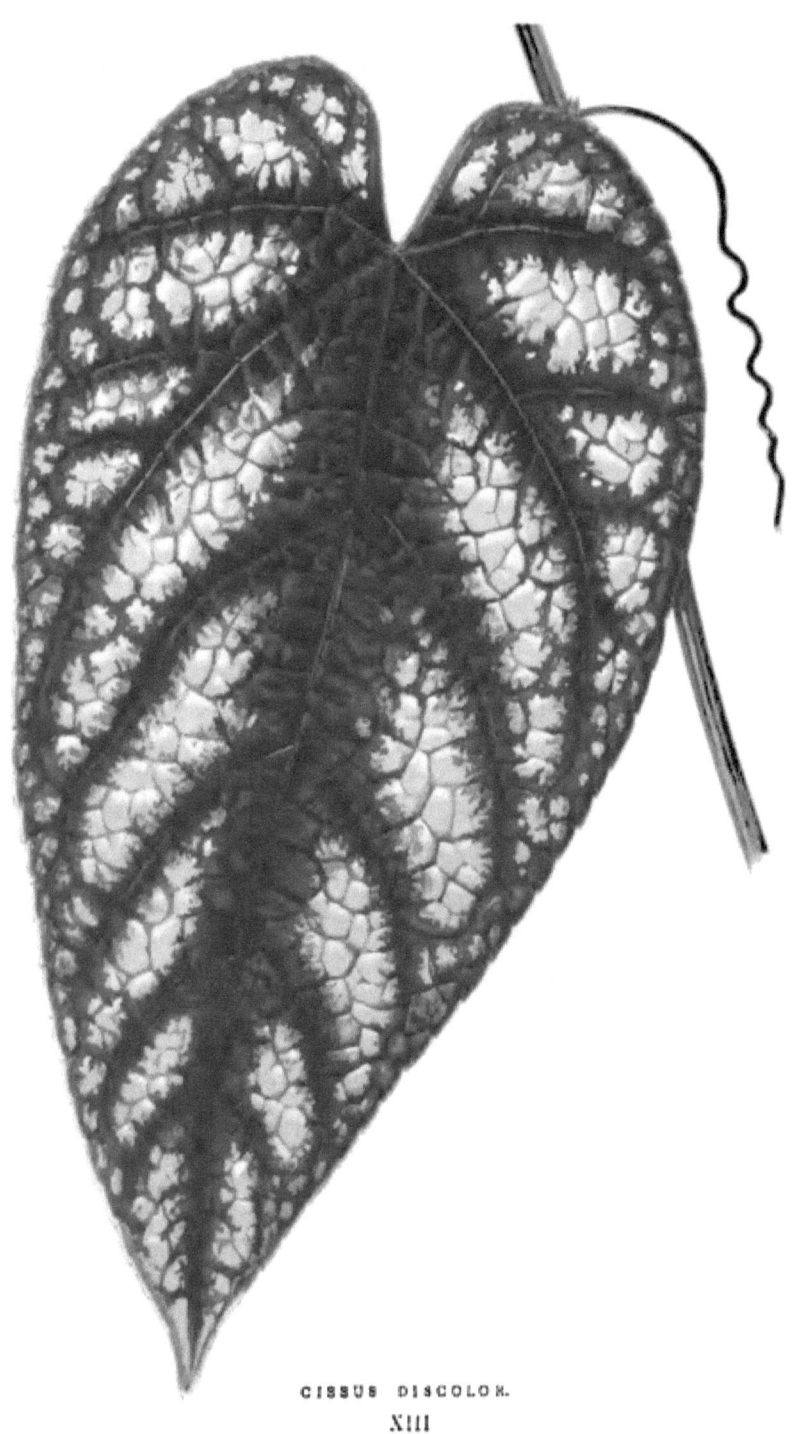

CISSUS DISCOLOR.
XIII

CISSUS DISCOLOR.

PLATE XIII.

> "The valley holds its Feast of Roses,
> That joyous time, when pleasures pour
> Profusely round, and in their shower
> Hearts open, like the Season's Rose—
> The Flow'ret of a hundred leaves,
> Expanding while the dew-fall flows,
> And every leaf its balm receives."
> Moore.

DERIVED from the Greek, *Kissus*—ivy. A genus of climbers, some of the species of which are very ornamental. Linnæus, 4, order 1, Natural Order *Vitaceæ*.

Cissus discolor was introduced into this country in 1851, by Messrs. Rollisson and Sons, of Tooting.

A climbing stove creeper, with somewhat ovate pointed or elongated heart-shaped leaves.

Native of Java.

The leaves, which are six inches long and two inches and a half broad, are coloured on the upper surface in the richest manner conceivable, the plant rivaling in its beautiful foliage the finest of the *Anœctochilus* family; the colour being a rich green, clouded with white, peach, and dark purplish crimson, and covered with a metallic lustre.

The under side of the leaf a rich brownish crimson. No description or painting can do justice to the beauty of these superb leaves when in perfection.

The mid-vein of the leaf, and the long-forked tendrils, (which are formed at the leaf-joints,) are crimson in colour.

Easily propagated, and the price having become very reasonable, every stove ought to possess this lovely plant.

Temperature, winter from 60° to 65°, summer from 70° to 75°.

Culture. Soil, a compost of sandy peat and strong fibry loam, with well-decomposed hot-bed or cow dung; this will suit the plant admirably. Being so rapid a grower it requires a rich soil. *Cissus discolor* can be used either as a suitable cover to the naked walls of a stove, even where nothing else will grow; or to train up pillars; or under pot-culture, on a balloon-shaped trellis.

This plant requires shading from the hot beams of the sun, or the rich colouring will fade quickly. Care should also be taken not to syringe the plant, as wherever water falls on the leaves it destroys the metallic lustre.

Propagation. By cuttings. Take young top shoots, removing the lowest leaves, and cut clean at a joint. Prepare a cutting pot, with bell-glass to fit, lay over the hole an oyster-shell or large piece of pot, and upon this a layer of small broken crocks, and above this a thin layer of moss, over which place as much of the above-mentioned compost as will fill the pot to within an inch of the rim; fill that inch with pure silver-sand. Give a gentle watering, and as soon as the water sinks and the sand is firm plant the cuttings, taking care to close the sand round each. Water again gently, and fit on the bell-glass. Plunge the pot in moderate bottom-heat, or set it on a heated surface of moist sand. Wipe the glass occasionally, and as soon as the cuttings are rooted pot off, and still continue to protect with a hand-glass until they are able to bear full exposure.

Fern treatment is suitable to *Cissus discolor*.

The illustration is from a plant in Mr. Howard's collection.

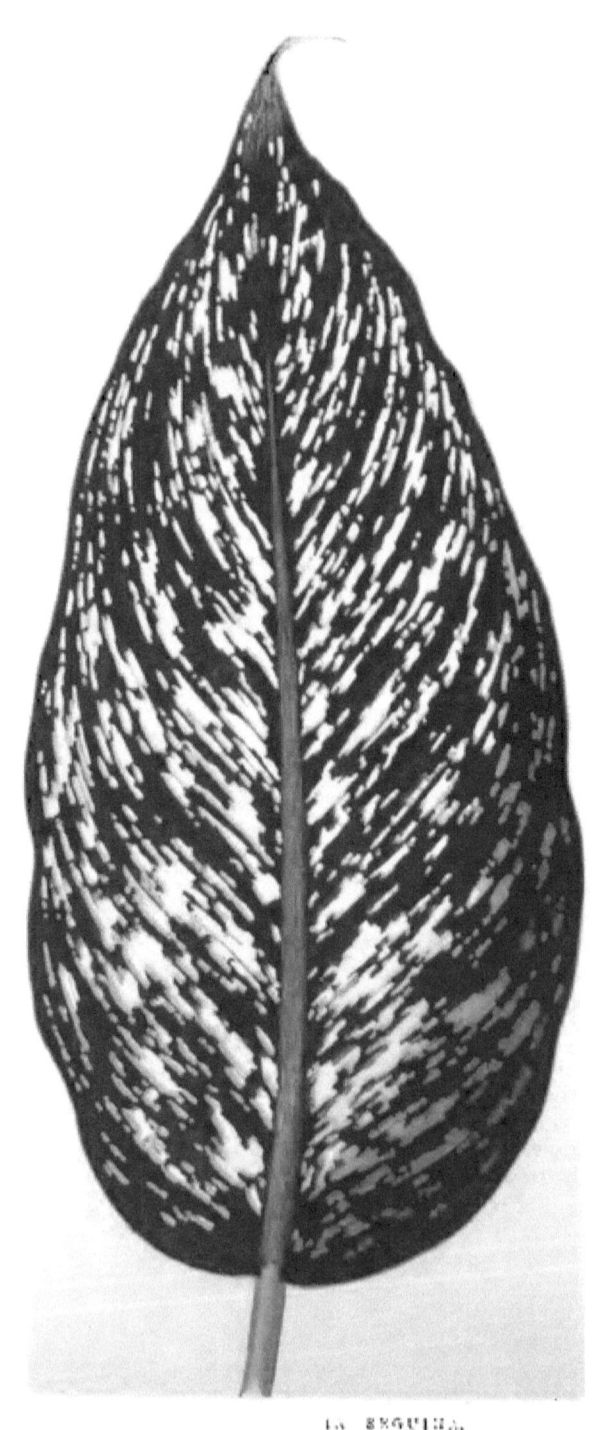

D. SEGUINA.
...ulata.
XIV

DIEFFENBACHIA SEGUINA.—Var. Maculata.

PLATE XIV.

> "Oh! could we wake from sorrow; were it all
> A troubled dream like this, to cast aside
> Like an untimely garment with the morn;
> Could the long fever of the heart be cool'd
> By a sweet breath from nature; or the gloom
> Of a bereaved affection pass away
> With looking on the lively tints of flowers—
> How lightly were the spirit reconciled
> To make this beautiful bright world its home."
> — WILLIS.

By some authors united with *Caladium.*

Dieffenbachia seguina is a native of South America.

It is said that this plant has the power, when chewed, of swelling the tongue and destroying the power of speech. Dr.

Hooker gives an instance of a man who lost the faculty of speech for several days, owing to incautiously chewing a bit of this plant.

The present variety was introduced into England in the year 1820.

A shrubby stove plant, growing to the height of four feet, bearing leaves more than a foot in length and five inches in width, and of a lengthy oval shape, having a pointed apex. The colour of the leaf is a very light green, dotted over with numberless irregular-shaped pure white blotches, giving the plant a decidedly variegated appearance; very striking even when among similar-coloured foliaged plants. It is a quick grower, and should be in every collection of beautiful-foliaged plants.

Culture. This species requires the heat of a moderate stove, and the white variegation becomes much purer in colour when grown close to the glass. Soil, strong fibry loam two parts, sandy peat one part, vegetable mould one part, the whole well mixed together with sand and a few pieces of charcoal. As the stems are very soft and fleshy no water should be thrown over the plant when at rest, or they will suddenly damp off. Pot in spring, and drain well.

Propagation. Large cuttings taken off above the stem, and potted singly in sand, placed on a heated surface, and having a hand-light over them, and kept shaded, will root without difficulty. As soon as they are rooted begin to give air and less shade. When the plants will bear full exposure, re-pot in the proper compost. Stop the shoots to cause a bushy habit, or else they will run up with naked unsightly stems.

For plants my thanks are due to Messrs. Veitch, of the Exotic Nursery, Chelsea, and to Mr. Rollisson, of Tooting.

The woodcut illustration is from a photograph of a plant in the author's collection.

BEGONIA REX.
Var. Nebulosa.
XV

BEGONIA REX.—Var. Nebulosa.

Rollisson.

Plate XV.

> "The bard of night, the angel of the spring,
> O'er the wild minstrels of the grove supreme,
> Near his betrothed flower expands his wing;
> Wake, lovely rose, awake, and hear thy poet sing!
> The night is past; wake, Queen of every flower,
> Breathing the soul of spring in thy perfume;
> The pearls of morning are thy wedding dower,
> Thy bridal garment is a robe of bloom!
> Wake, lovely flower! for now the winter's gloom
> Hath wept itself in April showers away;
> Wake, lovely flower! and bid thy smiles assume
> A kindred brightness with the rosy ray
> That streaks the floating clouds with the young blush of day."

Another of those beautiful seedlings raised in 1858, by Messrs. Rollisson, of Tooting.

The leaves of the variety in question are covered in clusters with white spots; in the centre of each spot is a single red hair, which gives the plant a very distinct appearance.

A stove herbaceous plant, with all its parts densely covered with a red pubescence.

For culture and propagation see *Begonia Rex* and its variety *grandis*.

I am indebted to Messrs. Rollisson, of Tooting, for a plant of this lovely *Begonia*.

SONERILA MARGARITACEA.
XVI

SONERILA MARGARITACEA.

PLATE XVI.

> "And now that there is something bright on earth,
> The clouds are driven from the clear blue sky,
> And Heaven is bright'ning too. Serene and calm,
> The very air is hushed into repose,
> That not a breath may ruffle the young flowers
> Now gently waking into life and light."
> Miss Twamley.

Linnæus, 8.—*Octandria*, 1.—*Monogynia*, natural order Melastomads, *(Melastomaceæ,)* small stove plants.

The *Sonerila Margaritacea* is a very handsome species.

A native of Java. Introduced in 1848.

Summer temperature 70° to 80°, winter 60° to 65°.

A half-shrubby low-growing plant, with numerous round shoots and small leaves, beautifully mottled all over the upper surface with silver spots.

The flowers are numerous, and of a pleasing rose-colour.

Propagation by cuttings in the spring. The cuttings must

be small, with not more than three or four leaves; the lower leaves should be cut off. Plant in sand, in a pot covered with a bell-glass, and plunge in heat. Shade from the sun's rays, and constantly wipe the glasses, as the cuttings are apt to damp off when in confined moisture. As soon as roots are formed pot off immediately, and again cover them with bell-glasses for a month, giving air daily to inure them to bear full exposure.

Summer management. In March re-pot the plants into pots two sizes larger, and re-pot again in June. Water moderately, but give plenty of atmospheric moisture during the season of growth. As soon as the flowers are half over cut them all off, buds and all, as an excess of bloom is almost sure to destroy this somewhat delicate gem. During the bright sunny days of midsummer the plants should be kept in a somewhat shady part of the stove. The plant is of free growth; under proper treatment a young plant will become a bush two feet through in a couple of years.

Winter management. During this season the plants should be kept very moderately watered, and fully exposed to the sun's rays, they should also be frequently turned round, so that every leaf may have its full share of light.

The illustration is from a specimen grown by Mr. Veitch, Royal Exotic Nursery, Chelsea.

MARANTA WARSZEWICZII.
XVII

MARANTA WARSCEWICZII.

PLATE XVII.

> "O LADY, leave thy silken thread
>   And flowery tapestrie,
> There's living roses on the bush,
>   And blossoms on the tree;
> Stoop where thou wilt, thy careless hand
>   Some random bud will meet;
> Thou canst not tread, but thou wilt find
>   The daisy at thy feet."
>
> Hood.

NATIVE country Central America. Introduced in 1854, by M. Warscewicz, and named after that botanist.

A strong-growing evergreen herb, requiring the heat of the stove; leaf-stem one foot high; leaves two feet long and six inches broad, having feathery stripes of a yellowish green on each side of the midrib, running parallel with the margin. This is a fine strong-foliaged species.

Culture. Quite as easy to grow as the old favourite *Maranta zebrina*. Soil, a rich compost of strong fibry loam, sandy peat, vegetable mould, and well-decomposed cow-dung, in equal parts, with a sprinkling of silver-sand; add a few large pieces of charcoal throughout the soil, and on the top of the drainage. This plant, when in a twelve-inch pot and in perfect health, is exceedingly ornamental. Heat 70° to 75° in summer, 60° to 65° in winter.

Propagation. Take off one or more side suckers, pot them in small pots in very sandy soil, and place under a handlight or frame in heat. These suckers will quickly make fresh roots, and may then be hardened off and afterwards re-potted, treating in the same manner as the parent plant.

The illustration is from a plant in the collection of Mr. Veitch, Royal Exotic Nursery, Chelsea.

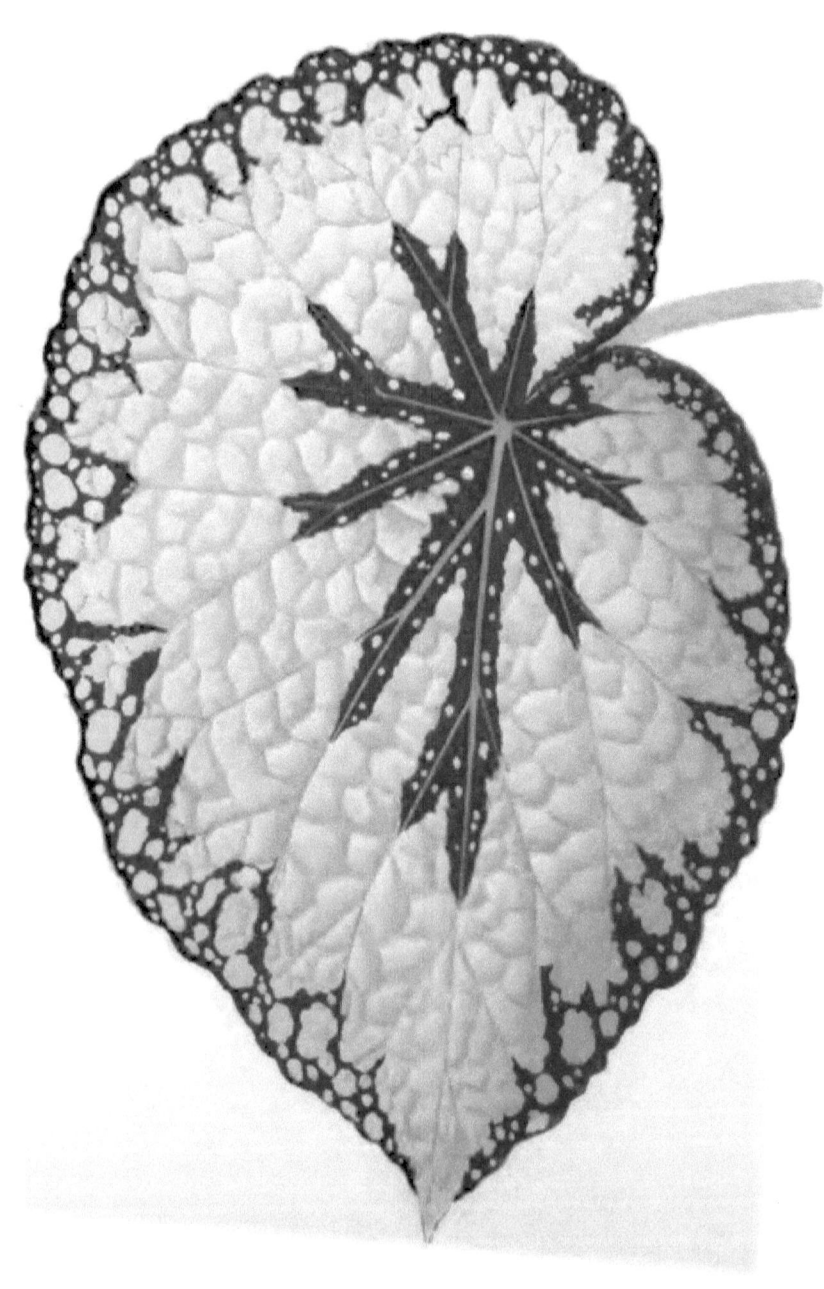

BEGONIA MARSHALLI.
XVIII

BEGONIA MARSHALLII.

PLATE XVIII.

"Oh! they look upward in every place
  Through this beautiful world of ours,
And dear as a smile on an old friend's face
  Is the smile of the bright, bright flowers!
They tell us of wanderings by woods and streams;
  They tell of the lanes and trees;
But the children of showers and sunny beams
  Have lovelier tales than these—
        The bright, bright flowers!"

THE plant now figured is another beautiful hybrid, between *Begonia Rex* and *B. splendida argentea*. It was raised by Mr. R. Franklin, gardener to James Garth Marshall, Esq., of Headingley Hall, near Leeds, and named after Mr. Marshall.

Mr. R. Fish, in the "Cottage Gardener," remarks that it is the finest of the numerous hybrids of the *Rex* breed he has yet seen, and that it may be ranked thus:—1.—*Begonia Marshallii*; 2.—*B. grandis*; 3.—*B. Rex*.

The leaves are nine inches long and six inches broad. A very broad band of silvery hue occupies the greater part of the leaf. In the very centre there are some long radiations of bright green, amongst which the silvery part meanders them; on the margin there is an edging of bright crimson hairs, and next that a kind of vandyking of green runs in and out of the silvered part. The leaf-stems are one foot long, and covered thinly with long white hairs.

B. Marshallii is propagated and grown in an exactly similar way to that of *B. Rex* already described, (page 17.)

It is astonishing how nature sports in her productions, and to what a state of perfection the art of gardening in the hybridizer's department has arrived. Will not other species of

Begonia sport! If they will, why not obtain scarlet bands from *Begonia sanguinea*, contrasted with the silvery white on the present variety. We throw this out as a hint to cultivators.

We are indebted to Mr. W. Cole, Nurseryman, Withington, near Manchester, for a leaf of this beautiful variety.

CALADIUM CRANTINI.
XIX

CALADIUM CHANTINI.

PLATE XIX.

"This day, said I, I will forget the world,
Its cares, and guilt, and passions, and will live
In sunshine and in beauty. So I went
Through fields and green bank'd lanes, where the spring flowers
Live on till summer. The short soft grass
Had caught a plenteous dew: the mountain herbs
Repaid my tread with sweet fragrance. Every hill
Put on a face of gladness; every tree
Shook its green leaves in joy: the meadows laugh'd;
The deep glen, where it caught the amber beams,
Began to draw its misty veil aside,
And smile and glisten through its pearly tear."

MIDSUMMER DAY DREAM.

NAMED in honour of M. Chantin, a French Nurseryman, who has introduced many new and rare plants.

Native country the banks of the Amazon River, in South America.

Introduced in 1857, by M. Chantin.

For an account of this genus see page 8, under *Caladium bicolor splendens*.

Description. A strong-growing, tuberous-rooted, stove herbaceous plant, with broad arrow-head-shaped leaves, fourteen inches long, by ten inches wide in the broadest part. The leaves are deep crimson in the centre, shading off to pale green towards the margin, and covered with a profusion of irregular shaped and sized white spots. Stem of the leaves two feet high, dark purple, striped with crimson. A splendid showy species, worthy of general cultivation.

Soil. Sandy loam, fibry peat, rotten cow-dung, and decayed leaf-mould, in equal parts, with a liberal addition of silver-sand. In using this compost it should be so dry that when a handful is taken up, and moderately pressed, and then allowed to drop, it will fall to pieces.

Culture. In the spring observe the tubers, and if the buds are beginning to sprout, it is time they should be re-potted. Turn the ball out of the old pot, and gently remove all last year's soil off the tubers, and also remove any dead roots, stems, etc.; examine the tuber to ascertain if it is quite sound; should any decaying spots appear, pare them quite smooth down to the sound part, and rub a little powdered chalk on the wounds, and then prepare a pot by well draining it with potsherds, and upon which place a layer of fibrous parts of the soil. Fill three fourths of the pot with prepared compost, and then plunge the pot on a tan-bed, or set it on a heated surface, and give a gentle watering, after which give no more water until the leaves begin to appear through the soil; after that gradually increase the quantity of water, and when the foliage is approaching its full size, water abundantly. If a thin layer of powdered charcoal is laid on the soil in the pot, the glowing colours of the leaves will be considerably heightened. In the autumn let the quantity of water be gradually diminished, and when the leaves quite decay withhold water altogether.

Propagation. It is propagated in the usual manner, by offsets from the old tuber. Take them off when a little advanced, and pot them in nearly pure sand till roots are emitted, then re-pot and treat as established plants, giving them a liberal quantity of liquid manure.

For plants of this magnificent species my thanks are due to Messrs. Rollisson, of Tooting, and Messrs. Jackson, of Kingston.

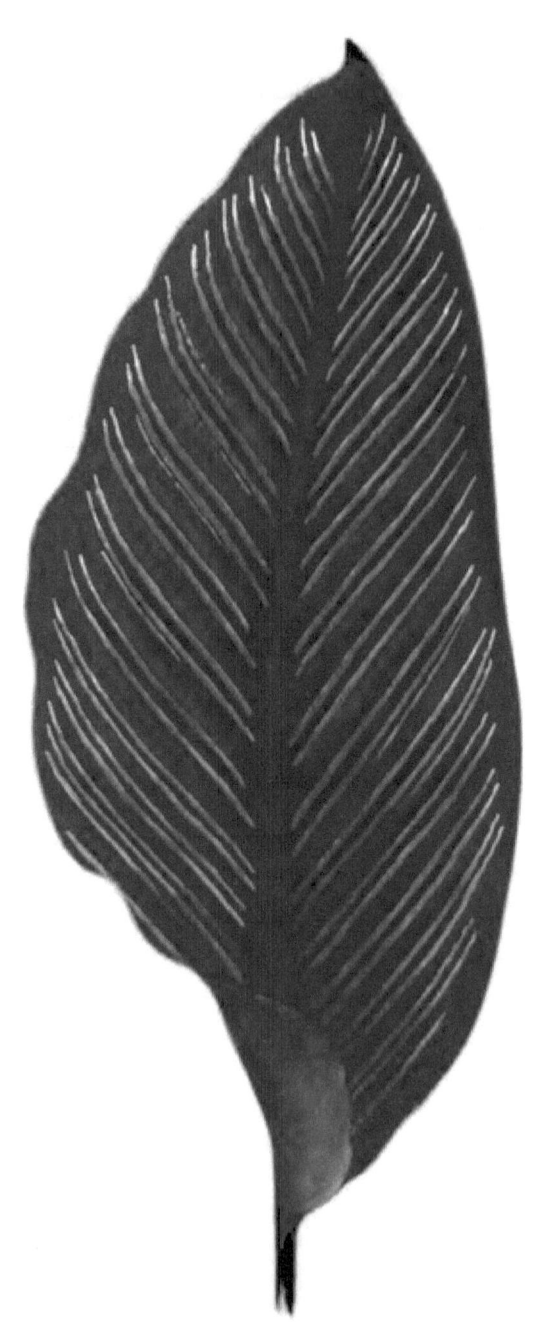

MARANTA REGALIS
XX

MARANTA REGALIS.

PLATE XX.

> "I bless Thy name,
> That Thou hast mantled the green earth with flowers,
> Linking our hearts to nature! By the love
> Of their wild blossoms, our young footsteps first
> Into her deep recesses are beguiled,
> Her minister cells, dark glen and forest bower.
> Amidst the low religious whisperings,
> The shivery leaf sounds of the solitude,
> The spirit wakes to worship, and is made
> Thy living temple."
>
> Mrs. Hemans.

Native country Columbia.

Introduced into the Royal Gardens, Kew, in 1854.

Maranta is named after B. Maranti, a Venetian physician and botanist, who lived about three hundred years ago. Natural order *Marantaceæ*, (Marants.) Stove plants from the West Indies, South America, Brazil, Guiana, East Indies, and Caraccas. The root of *Maranta arundinacea* is considered (in the East) a delicate article of food. The plant known as *Maranta Warscewiczii*, (Plate XVII., page 35,) is, more properly speaking, a *Calathea*, (see Plate I., page 1.)

Description. A stove plant with persistent leaves. Leaf-stalks a foot long, leaves oval-shaped, nine inches long and three inches broad; red underneath, green on the upper side, with two bright carmine linear lines between each vein across the leaf, changing when old to white. A strong plant will have a dozen or more of these beautiful leaves. It is one of the finest beautiful-foliaged plants ever introduced into this country, and not taking up much room, ought to be in every collection.

Culture. Soil a compost of fibrous loam, sandy peat, and

vegetable mould in equal parts, and a liberal addition of silver-sand, and a few bits of charcoal. The pots should be well drained, and in size proportioned to that of the plant. It must never be over-potted, or it will not have the leaves so correctly marked. The month of March is the best season for re-potting. The plants should be kept rather in the shade, for the sun takes out the colouring of the red stripes. Heat, summer 75° to 80°; winter 65° to 70°. In the summer water moderately, and in winter still less, for the roots will decay with too much water.

Propagation. When it is desired to increase the plant to the utmost, it should be shaken out of the soil, and divided into as many parts as the plant will make, but each part should have roots to it. If, however, it is desirable to keep one plant strong, then take off only one sucker with roots. Put these divisions into small pots, and place them under a hand-light in bottom heat in the stove, shading for a fortnight, then give a little air, and less shade, till the plants will bear full exposure; after which place them in a shady part of the stove, and re-pot as they need it. It is not difficult of propagation by this method.

For plants my thanks are due to Messrs. Rollisson, of Tooting, and Messrs. Jackson, of Kingston.

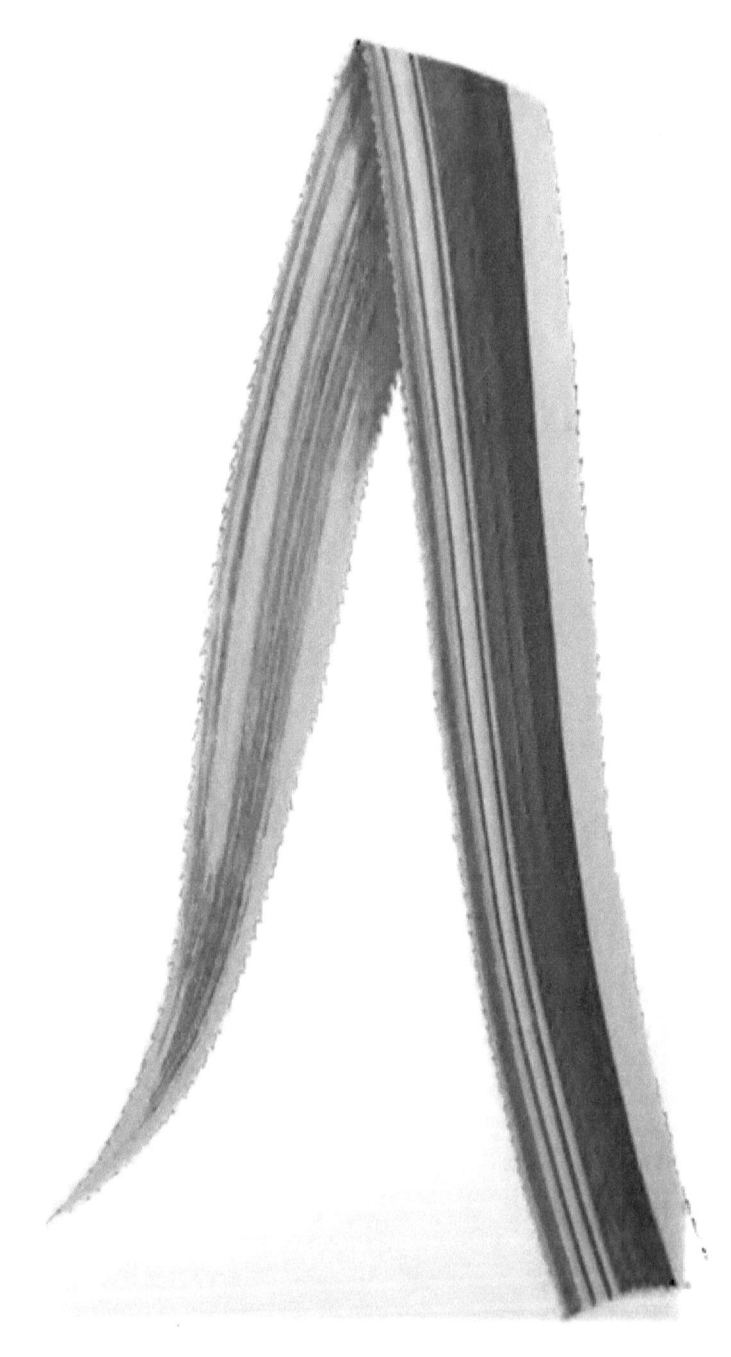

ANANASSA SATIVA VARIEGATA.
XXI

ANANASSA SATIVA VARIEGATA.

PLATE XXI.

> "The welcome flowers are blossoming,
>   In joyous troops reveal'd;
> They lift their dewy buds and bells
>   In garden, mead, and field.
> They lurk in every sunless path
>   Where forest children tread;
> They dot like stars the sacred turf
>   Which lies above the dead.
> They sport with every playful wind
>   That stirs the blooming trees,
> And laugh on every fragrant bush,
>   All full of toiling bees.
> From the green marge of lake and stream,
>   Fresh vale and mountain sod,
> They look in gentle glory forth—
>   The pure sweet flowers of God."
>
> GILBORNE LYONS.

The above plant is a variegated variety of the Pine-apple.

The name is derived from *Nanas*, the local Guiana name for the South American Pine-apple. Linnæus, 6.—*Hexandria*, 1.—*Monogynia*, Natural Order *Bromeliaceæ*, (Bromelworts.)

The plants that yield this most delicious of fruits were first cultivated, so as to bear fruit, in England, in 1715, at Richmond, the country seat of Sir Matthew Dickson. The Pine-apple was, however, introduced into this country as early as 1690. There are now as many as thirty distinct kinds, yet not above half a score of them are worthy of cultivation. Of these may be mentioned the Queen, an early sort, a free grower, and an excellent fruiter; the Ripley Queen, considered by some preferable to the last; Black Jamaica, the best winter pine; White Providence, the largest and noblest of the tribe, but inferior in quality; the Black Antigua, a splendid pyramidal fruit; St. Vincent or Green Olive, a good winter fruit; Brown

Sugar-loaf, a large juicy sort; Lemon Queen, Trinidad, Enville, etc.; the latter second-rate fruit.

When this beautiful variety was first introduced is unknown.

A stove herbaceous plant, with leaves from two to three feet long, having beautiful golden yellow and white stripes, the edge of each leaf being thickly covered with recurved spines.

Culture. Like the Pine-apple, this variety requires rather a strong compost, consisting of fibry loam two parts, well-decomposed dung half a part, and decayed leaves one part. Add to this a small quantity of peat, which will preserve the variegation and render the colours more vivid. Drain well and lay a thin layer of charcoal on the top of the drainage. Pot in March, and again in August, and a fine plant will be obtained quickly. Plunge the pot in a moderate-heated tan-bed, or a bed of leaves in the stove, and renew the heat as it fails by adding fresh tan or leaves. The plant, however, will grow and thrive in a high temperature without being plunged.

Propagation. Like the Common Pine-apple, this variety is increased from suckers which spring from the axils of the lower leaves. When these have attained a good size they should be separated from the parent, and allowed to dry up the wound at the base for twenty-four hours before planting. Then insert them in the tan or leaf-bed until fresh roots are formed; after which pot, and plunge in bottom-heat; give no water for a week or ten days, and then very little, (only just enough to keep the soil moist.) As soon as roots are emitted the quantity of water may be increased.

This variety bears a fruit of very inferior flavour, which generally produces a crown. When the fruit is ripe this crown may be twisted out of the fruit and treated as a sucker, and will mostly make a handsome plant.

Heat required 70° to 80° in summer, 60° to 65° in winter. In the latter season much less water is requisite.

The illustration is from Mr. Howard's plant.

CALADIUM ARGYRITES.
XXII

CALADIUM ARGYRITES.

PLATE XXII.

> Bring flowers, fresh flowers, for the bride to wear!
> They were born to blush in her shining hair;
> She is leaving the home of her childhood's mirth,
> She hath bid farewell to her father's hearth;
> Her place is by another's side—
> Bring flowers for the locks of the fair young bride!
>
> Bring flowers to the shrine where we kneel at prayer,
> They are nature's offering, their place is *there!*
> They speak of hope to the fainting heart,
> With a voice of promise they come and part;
> They sleep in the dust in wintry hours,
> Then break forth in glory—bring flowers, bright flowers!
> Mrs. Hemans.

For a description of this genus refer to *Caladium bicolor*, page 7.

Native country the banks of the Amazon River, in South America.

Introduced in 1857, by M. Chantin, a Nurseryman near Paris.

Description. A lovely, tuberous-rooted, stove herbaceous perennial, with arrow-head-shaped leaves, of small size. Ground light green, with white centre, and margins of the same; the rest of the leaf irregularly spotted with white. This is a gem of its kind, very beautiful, and well worthy of general cultivation.

Soil. Sandy peat and decayed leaves in equal parts, with a liberal addition of silver-sand.

Culture during the growing-season. This season commences about the end of March; at this time observe the tubers, and as soon as the first symptoms of growth are visible, take the pots to the potting-bench, turn out the ball, and carefully remove the soil from the tubers, clean away all decayed roots and old stems, and observe that the tubers are quite sound. If any mouldy or decaying spots appear, remove them by scraping the parts, after which apply a little powdered chalk to the wounds. Prepare a pot of a proportionate size to the tubers, drain it particularly well, and cover the drainage with a layer of turfy peat, and fill the pot to within an inch with the above compost; place the tuber upon it, and pack more compost round it, allowing the top to be just covered; give a gentle watering to settle the mould, and place in a heat of from 60° to 65°. As soon as the young leaves appear give a little more tepid water, but be careful not to give too much; the quantity may be increased as the plant advances in growth, but it should never be saturated. If a bell-glass is placed over the plant it adds considerably to its beauty, and assists the expansion of the leaves. The whole plant, as yet, has never exceeded nine inches in length.

Culture during the next period. In autumn, when the leaves begin to decay, gradually reduce the quantity of water, and when the plant is completely at rest place the pot in a warm place, and keep the soil just moist. Through the winter the tubers should be frequently examined, and, if shrinking too much, give a very little water, to keep them plump and fresh till the buds begin to swell in spring; then re-pot as directed above.

Propagation. The tubers, when large enough, send out smaller tubers at their sides; take one or more of these off, and after drying a little, in order to heal the wound, these tubers may be placed in a small pot, and treated afterwards the same as the parent plant.

For plants my thanks are due to Messrs. Rollisson, of Tooting, and Jackson, of Kingston.

MARANTA FASCIATA.

PLATE XXIII.

I love to go forth ere the dawn, to inhale
The health-breathing freshness that floats in the gale;
When the thorn and the woodbine are bursting with buds,
And the throstle is heard in the depths of the woods;
When the verdure grows bright where the rivulets run,
And the primrose and daisy look up at the sun.
At meridian I love to revisit the bowers,
'Mid the murmur of bees and the breathing of flowers,
When the boughs of the orchard with fruitage incline,
And the clusters are ripe on the stem of the vine.
I love too at evening to rest in the dell,
Where the tall fern is drooping above the green well;
When the vesper-star burns, when the zephyr-wind blows,
And the lay of the nightingale ruffles the rose.
There is a harvest of knowledge in all that I see,
For a stone or a leaf is a treasure to me.

J. C. Prince.

For a description of this genus refer to *Maranta regalis*, page 41.

Native country Brazil. Introduced in 1857, by M. Linden, a continental nurseryman, to whom we are much indebted for many of our beautiful ornamental-foliaged plants.

Description. A half-shrubby stove plant, with leaves nearly heart-shaped, eight inches long by six inches wide at the broadest part. Upper side green, with broad bands of white, reaching nearly across, from the midrib to the margin. Underneath green, slightly shaded with purplish crimson. A very distinct, new, and beautiful species. Flowers non vidi.

Culture. Requires a warm stove constantly. Heat 75° to 80° in summer, 70° to 75° in winter. Soil fibry loam, sandy peat, and well decomposed vegetable mould in equal parts, adding silver-sand liberally, and a few small pieces of charcoal.

Let the pots be well drained. Pot in March, and water freely during the summer months, but moderately in winter.

Propagation. Young shoots that rise from the sides, taken off in spring, and planted in sand in well-drained pots, placed under a bell-glass or a handlight, will root. The glass must be frequently wiped, or the cuttings will damp off; shade from bright sun, or the cuttings will flag and perish. As soon as roots are emitted the plants must be potted into small pots in a very sandy compost, and replaced under the handlight, and kept close for a short time, till they begin to grow; then gradually inure them to bear the full sun and air, after which re-pot, and treat the same as with older plants. It is a difficult plant to propagate, requiring constant attention to shading, and wiping the wet off the glass.

For plants my thanks are due to Messrs. Veitch, of Chelsea, and Messrs. Rollisson, of Tooting.

ANŒCTOCHILUS SETACEUS (AUREUS.)

BRISTLY ANŒCTOCHILUS.

PLATE XXIV.

> I know a bank whereon the wild thyme blows,
> Where oxlips and the nodding violet grows,
> Quite over-canopied with luscious woodbine,
> With sweet musk-roses, and with eglantine:
> There sleeps Titania, some time of the night,
> Lulled in these flowers with dances and delight.
> MIDSUMMER NIGHT'S DREAM.

For a description of this genus see page 13.

Native country Ceylon. Introduced to Kew Gardens in 1836.

Description. A stove orchidaceous plant, the leaves of which are its great recommendation to the cultivator. The flowers, though exceedingly curious in their structure, are not showy, but the leaves are really most lovely. The ground colour is a dark velvety green tinge, with a metallic lustre. The whole surface intersected, as it were, with a network of golden reddish lines. Examined with a microscope when the sun is shining full upon the leaf, the veins appear rich beyond description. Then also the form of the leaf, and the dwarf neat habit of the plant, render it one of the most beautiful objects in nature.

Culture. This plant is found in shady places, growing on decomposed leaves and the debris of rocks, hence in culture a similar soil should be used. Cultivators have discovered that the plant thrives well in sphagnum moss, mixed with broken pots and silver-sand, covered with a bell-glass, and shaded from mid-day sun in summer. Others grow them in lumpy sandy peat, and placed under a kind of frame in the stove, covered with large loose squares of greenish glass. The advantage of this mode is, that when the moisture is condensed on the inner side of the glass, the squares can be carefully lifted off and turned. All, however, that seems to be necessary, is to place in a shady close atmosphere, and to pot in a light open soil, that will allow the thick fleshy roots to run freely amongst it. Water must be very sparingly given, because too much rots off these fleshy woolly roots directly.

Propagation. The plant sends forth suckers from the base of the stem. When these have put out a root or two divide them carefully from the parent; pot them in the compost, in small pots, draining well, and place under bell-glasses until fairly established; then re-pot, and treat them similarly to the old plants.

They require a high temperature—75° to 80° in summer, and 60° to 65° in winter. Give more water in summer, and very moderately in winter.

The plant for illustration was furnished by Mr. Howard, of Roselands, Enfield.

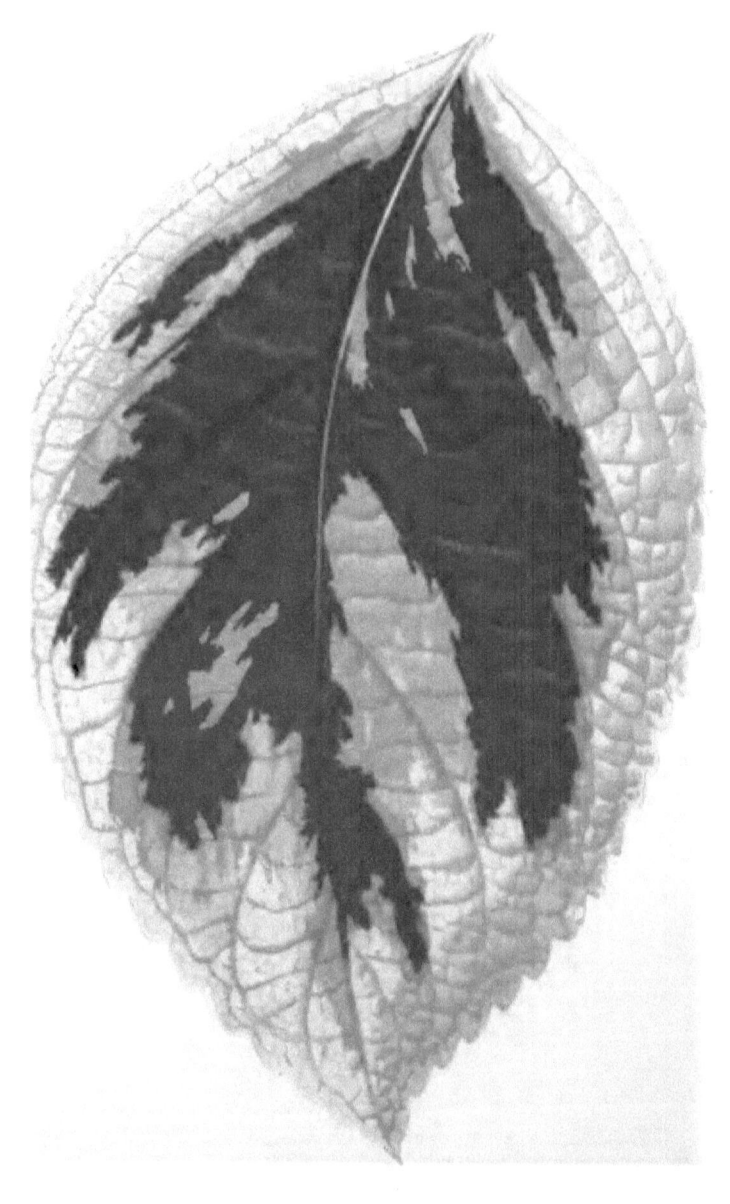

AUCUBA JAPONICA VARIEGATA.

HYDRANGEA JAPONICA · VARIEGATA.

PLATE XXV.

I WANDER'D lonely as a cloud
That floats on high o'er vales and hills,
When all at once I saw a crowd,
A host of golden daffodils,
Beside a lake, beneath the trees,
Fluttering and dancing in the breeze.
The waves beside them danced, but they
Out-did the sparkling waves in glee:
A poet could not but be gay
In such a jocund company;
I gazed, and gazed, but little thought
What wealth the show to me had brought.
For oft, when on the couch I lie,
In vacant or in pensive mood,
They flash upon that inward eye
Which is the bliss of solitude;
And then my heart with pleasure fills,
And dances with the daffodils.
WORDSWORTH.

Hydrangea is a genus of dwarf deciduous shrubs, which, when in bloom, are very showy. The name is derived from the Greek, *hydor*—water, and *aggeion*—a vessel, because the capsule of a portion of the species somewhat resembles a cup. The various species are natives of Virginia, Carolina, Florida, China, and Nepal. Linnæus, 10—*Decandria*, 2.—*Digynia*. Natural order *Hydrangyaceæ*, (Hydrangeads.)

The present species from Japan, was introduced in 1843, and the variegated variety was raised by M. Van Houtte, Nurseryman, Ghent, and sent to this country by him in 1851.

Description. Leaves ovate, oblong, serrated at the margin, and beautifully blotched and margined with white. Plant, a deciduous shrub, with woody stems and rather straggling habit; decidedly an acquisition to the class of beautiful foliaged plants. The flowers are also very handsome, and of a blue and white colour.

Culture. Requires the protection of the greenhouse, and a sandy loam. The species thrives better with dung and leaf-mould added, but the variety with coloured leaves must have a poor soil, or the variegation will disappear in a great measure. Summer temperature $55°$ to $60°$, winter temperature $45°$ to $50°$.

Propagation. Cuttings of the young wood, taken off in May, planted in sand, and placed in a gentle heat closely shaded from the sun, will root in a month, or even less, if a good heat is kept up in the frame or propagating house. As soon as the cuttings are rooted pot them off singly into three-inch pots, and re-place them in heat and shade till fresh growth is attained; then give them more air and light, and in six weeks after re-pot without disturbing the bulbs. They will then bear full exposure in the greenhouse, though they will grow faster and be more variegated if kept in a moderately-heated stove during the summer. Large plants may be quickly obtained by frequent re-pottings into larger pots. Let the shoots be topped when the plants are small, in order to have dense bushy specimens, covered with their finely-variegated foliage.

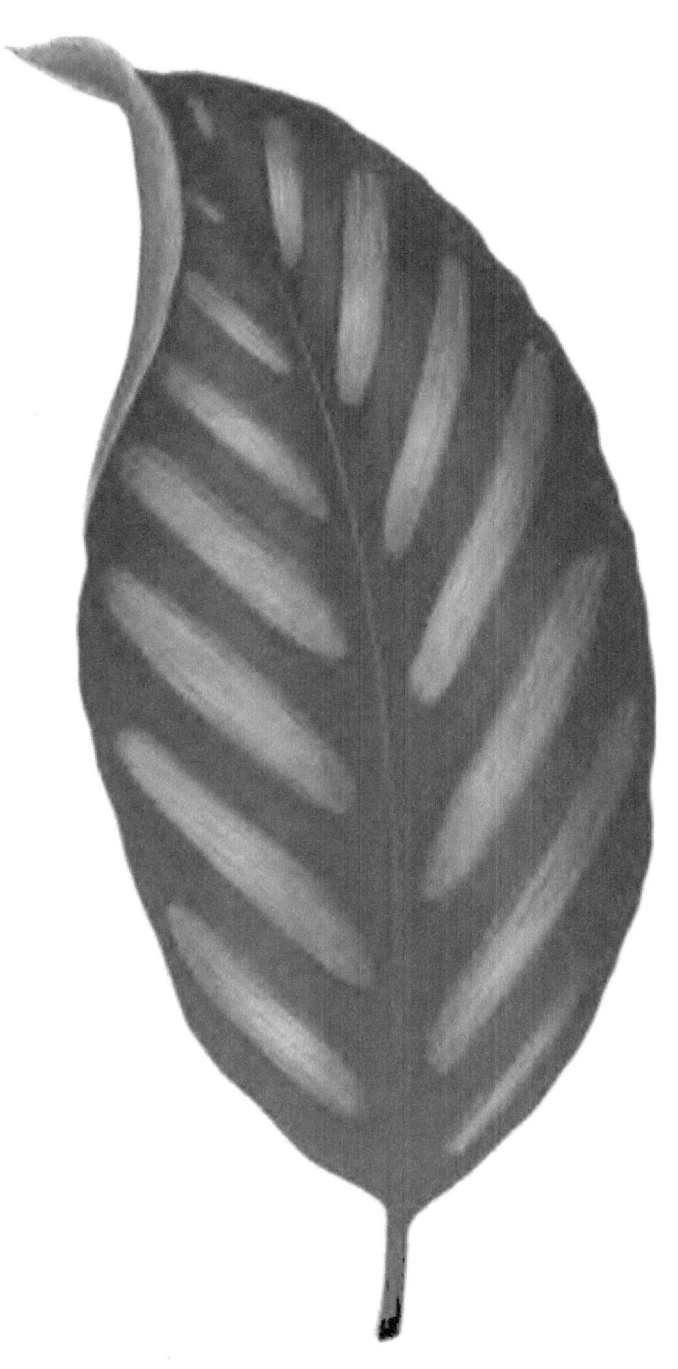

MARANTA PORTEANA.
XXVI

MARANTA PORTEANA.

PLATE XXVI.

> Dost love sweet hyacinth? Its scented leaf
> Curls manifold,—all love's delights blow double;
> 'T is said this flow'ret is inscribed with grief—
> But let that hint of a forgotten trouble.
> I pluck'd the primrose at night's dewy noon;
> Like Hope, it shew'd its blossoms in the night;
> 'T was, like Endymion, watching for the Moon!
> And here are Sun-flowers, amorous of light!
> These golden buttercups are April's seal,—
> These daisy stars her constellations be;
> These grow so lowly, I was forced to kneel,
> Therefore I pluck no daisies but for thee!
> Here's daisies for the morn, primrose for gloom,
> Pansies and roses for the noontide hours:—
> A wight once made a dial of their bloom,—
> So may thy life be measured out by flowers!
> Hood.

This handsome species was introduced in 1858, by M. Linden, Nurseryman, Brussels.

Native country Brazil.

Description. A handsome stove perennial, of a neat compact habit, and very beautiful foliage. The leaves are smooth, shining, oblong in shape, and sharp-pointed; colour a green ground, striped with white on the upper surface, and a self purple on the under side. Quite distinct from *Maranta fasciata*, and equally beautiful and worthy of cultivation.

Culture. Like all the rest of the genus, this species requires a stove temperature of 70° to 80° in summer, and of 60° to 65° in winter.

Soil. A compost of sandy loam, fibry peat, and leaf-mould in equal parts, with a free admixture of silver-sand, to keep it free and open, with a sprinkling of charcoal or small crocks. Pot in March, and drain well, using two sizes larger every shift.

If a tan-bed is convenient and of a moderate temperature, or, lacking this, bottom-heat from hot water, the plants will thrive better if they are plunged half-way up the pot in this warmth immediately after potting.

Propagation. When the plants have attained a good size they send up side suckers; as soon as these suckers have made roots pass a knife blade between the main plant and each sucker, and then carefully upheave them. Pot immediately in a proportionate-sized pot, and in the above compost; plunge in bottom-heat, placing a handlight or bell-glass over, and shade from the bright sunshine. These suckers will soon push forth fresh leaves and roots, after which they must be gradually inured to bear full exposure to the light and air. Then re-pot, and treat as the parent plant.

The plant illustrated was furnished by Messrs. Rollisson, of Tooting.

APHELANDRA LEOPOLDI.
XXVII

APHELANDRA LEOPOLDI.

PRINCE LEOPOLD'S APHELANDRA.

PLATE XXVII.

Grass for our cattle to devour
He makes the growth of every field;
Herbs for man's use, of various pow'r,
That either food or physic yield.
With cluster'd grapes He crowns the vine
To cheer man's heart oppress'd with cares;
Gives oil that makes his face to shine,
And corn that wasted strength repairs.
The trees of God, without the care
Or art of man, with sap are fed;
The mountain cedars look as fair
As those in royal gardens bred.
How various, Lord, Thy works are found,
For which Thy wisdom we adore!
The earth is with Thy treasure crown'd,
Till nature's hand can grasp no more.

Psalm civ.

The *Aphelandras* are stove evergreen shrubs, allied to *Justicia*, and having handsome flowers. Linnæus, 14.—*Didynamia*, 2.—*Angiospermia*. Natural order *Acanthaceæ*, (Acanthads.)

Native country of *Aphelandra Leopoldi*, South America. Introduced, in 1854, to the Ghent Nurseries.

Description. A stove shrub, of great beauty, both in foliage and florescence; the leaves are opposite and broadly lanceolate, six inches long, and two and a half broad in the centre, deep green, with distinct pure white veins running from the midrib to the margin. Flowers terminal, in compact spikes, and of a yellow colour. Habit inclined to run up with a single stem.

Culture. It requires a compost of rough peat and fibry loam in equal parts, with a small admixture of leaf-mould and plenty of silver-sand, to keep the compost free and open. Pot in March, and drain well, with broken pots and pieces of charcoal on the top of the drainage. In summer water freely, but in winter moderately. Pinch off the leading shoot in spring, to cause side-shoots to push forth, and stop these again during the summer, to make more shoots, so as to form a compact dense bush.

Summer temperature 70° to 80°, winter 55° to 60°.

A moist atmosphere during the growing season is necessary, to encourage the full development of the fine foliage and bright colours.

Propagation. Short side-shoots make the best cuttings, and early spring is the best season for this work. Plant the cuttings with the leaves entire in clean sand. Cover them with a bell-glass, and set the pot of cuttings on a heated surface, or, what is better, plunge it in a warm tan-bed. Shade from sunshine, and keep the sand just moist, and wipe the bell-glass every day for the first fortnight. By this time the roots will begin to push forth, when a little air must be given every evening till growth appears. Then pot off the rooted cuttings, and place in a very shady part of the stove. Afterwards gradually inure them to bear full exposure, re-pot, and treat them the same as the old plants.

For a plant my thanks are due to Messrs. Rollisson, of Tooting.

POTHOS ARGYRAEA.
XXVIII

POTHOS ARGYRÆA.

PLATE XXVIII.

> Bright and glorious is that revelation,
> Written all over this great world of ours,
> Making evident our own creation
> In these stars of earth,—these golden flowers.
> Gorgeous flowerets in the sunlight shining,
> Blossoms flaunting in the eye of day,
> Tremulous leaves, with soft and silver lining,
> Buds that open only to decay:
> Everywhere about us they are glowing,—
> Some like stars to tell us spring is born;
> Others, their blue eyes with tears o'erflowing,
> Stand like Ruth amid the golden corn.
> In all places, then, and in all seasons,
> Flowers expand their light and sunlike wings,
> Teaching us, by most persuasive reasons,
> How akin they are to human things.
>   LONGFELLOW.

Pothos, natural order Orontiads, *(Orontiaceæ.)* Linnæus, 4.—*Tetandria*, 1.—*Magynia*. Allied to *Anthurium*.

Native country Borneo.

Introduced in 1857, by Mr. Thomas Lobb, to Messrs. Veitch and Son, Royal Exotic Nursery, Chelsea.

Description. It is quite a gem, of remarkably neat and compact habit, and almost rivalling in beauty some of the *Anœctochilus* family. The leaves are obliquely-ovate in shape, are of a rich green, blotched with silvery white, with an irregular band of the latter colour running along the centre rib. It is a beautiful plant, and will be a great favourite in all collections of beautiful foliaged plants. This species has not yet flowered in this country that we know of.

Culture. Summer temperature 75° to 80°, winter 65° to 70°. Soil, sandy fibry peat—half, decayed leaves and fibry loam in equal parts; the whole mixed with small pieces of charcoal and silver-sand.

Pot in March, taking care that the pots are clean and well drained: re-pot again as soon as the roots shew through the crocks at the bottom of the pot, and the pot begins to get full of roots. If a large plant is required, it may soon be obtained by frequently potting as the roots are found to fill the pot. Whilst growing give a liberal supply of water, but in winter water very moderately, and do not at any time wet the leaves.

This beautiful species may also be grown as a basket plant: the shoots should be pegged down and made to droop downwards. When grown in pots or in baskets this plant should be securely shaded from the bright sunshine, inasmuch as the glowing light causes the silvery blotches to become of a pale green colour.

We can confidently recommend this singular and beautiful gem as well worthy of general cultivation.

Propagation. Young tops taken off and placed in a cutting pot, watering after they are put in to settle the sand about them, and placed in heat under a handlight or bell-glass, they strike very easily. As soon as roots are emitted pot them off at once in the above compost, replacing them in their former quarters, and shade for a few days from the sun: then gradually inure them to bear full exposure to the sun.

For the present specimen my thanks are due to Mr. Veitch, Jun., of the Exotic Nursery, Chelsea.

XXIX

DRACÆNA FERREA.

PLATE XXIX.

"Ah! if so much of beauty
Pour itself into each vein
Of life and of creation,
How beautiful must the
Great fountain be—
The bright, the Eternal."

For a description of the genus see page 6.

Native country China. Introduced in 1771.

Description. Another tall stove shrub, growing erect, with few side branches. Flowers white, not showy. Leaves a foot long, and four inches wide, of a long oval shape, and entire at the margin. Colour a uniform dark reddish purple, both sides coloured alike. The very distinct colouring of the leaves renders this plant a very striking object in a collection.

Culture. Requires the heat of a warm stove. Summer temperature 70° to 80°, winter 65° to 70°. Soil, strong fibrous loam, mixed with small pieces of charcoal and a sprinkling of silver-sand. The pots should be well drained. Re-pot every spring, taking off as much of the old soil as possible, without injuring the roots, and place the plants in the full light of the sun as much as possible, in order to bring out the full colour.

Propagation. Take a tall plant with a naked stem, cut it down to within four inches of the soil, then cut the stem into pieces two inches long, and plant these pieces in sandy soil, covering them half an inch above the top. Plunge the pot in a strong bottom-heat, giving but little water: each division will soon send up a shoot, and emit roots. Pot them off, preserving the roots carefully, and place them under a handlight until they begin to grow again; then harden off gradually, and re-pot as they require it. The top, with a few of the lower leaves taken off, may be put in sand under a bell-glass, plunged in heat, and will the soonest make a good-sized plant.

For a plant my thanks are due to Messrs. Rollisson, of Tooting.

ANŒCTOCHILUS ELATUS.
XXX

ANŒCTOCHILUS STRIATUS.

STRIPED ANŒCTOCHILUS.

PLATE XXX.

> "Oh, there are curious things of which men know
> As yet but little! secrets lying hid
> Within all natural objects. Be they shells,
> Which ocean flingeth forth from off her billows
> On the low sand, or flowers, or trees, or grasses,
> Covering the earth; rich metals or bright ores,
> Beneath the surface. He who findeth out
> Those secret things hath a fair right to gladness;
> For he hath well performed, and doth awake
> Another note of praise on nature's harp
> To hymn her great Creator."

The present plant is another of those little gems of the *Anœctochilus* family.

Native countries Ceylon and Borneo.

Introduced by Mr. Rae, to Kew, in 1840.

Description. The leaves of this genus are acknowledged to be the most beautiful of foliage known, and the present species is fully as handsome as any of this interesting family, and moreover it is the most distinct. The leaves are oblong-linear, dark bronzy green in colour, slightly veined, and having broad distinct stripes of ochreous yellow extending along the centre of each leaf. The plant is rather small, and has a tendency to grow up with a short stem.

Culture. Like all the genus, this species must be grown under a bell-glass or in a close frame. The soil should be a mixture of fibrous peat and sphagnum moss, chopped small and freely mixed with silver-sand, having a few small pieces of charcoal added. It is essential that the pots should be remarkably well drained, because stagnant water is certain death to the plant. A remarkable fact has just come under our notice, a fact bearing upon the amount of cold these plants will bear without injury. A friend had a plant of *Anœctochilus xanthophyllus* given to him last September, (1859:) he had no stove to put it into, nor even a bell-glass to cover it with. The plant was potted in the above compost, in a well-drained pot, into which four or five sticks were thrust close to the sides, and tied at the top, forming, as it were, the ribs of a tent, over which a piece of newspaper was tied, and the plant placed in a greenhouse, in the warmest part. In this situation it remained until January, and although the temperature in the severe frosts of November and December frequently fell as low as 35° in the greenhouse, yet this supposed eminently tender plant did not suffer in the least degree, and has not as yet lost any of its leaves. This accidental experiment proves that many plants will exist in a much lower temperature than that of their native country.

Propagation. By taking off a rooted sucker, which the plant sends up occasionally, or pegging down the plant, and when it throws out roots, cutting them off at the joint below. Pot in the above compost, and place them on a gentle bottom-heat in a close frame, or under a bell-glass, till fresh roots are emitted, giving no water or air for the first few weeks. Pay particular attention to wiping the glasses whenever any moisture is condensed on the inside. After a new growth has taken place, remove the plants, and place them amongst the others of its tribe, re-potting occasionally in April.

The illustration is from a plant kindly forwarded by Mr. Joseph Sidley, gardener to Samuel Ashton, Esq., Godley Hyde, near Manchester.

POINSETTIA PULCHERRIMA.
XXXI

POINSETTIA PULCHERRIMA.

MOST BEAUTIFUL POINSETTIA.

PLATE XXXI.

> Stars come forth when night her shroud
> Draws as daylight fainteth;
> Only on the tearful cloud
> God His glory painteth.
> Sweetest gleam the morning flowers
> When in tears they waken;
> Earth enjoys refreshing showers
> When the boughs are shaken.
> Flowers, by heedless footsteps press'd,
> All their sweets surrender;
> Gold must brook the fiery test.
> Ere it shews it splendour.

The *Poinsettia pulcherrima* of Graham is a solitary species of this genus, named in honour of M. Poinsette, the discoverer.

Linnæus, 21.—*Monœcia*, 1.—*Monandria*. Natural order *Spurgeworts*, (*Euphorbiaceæ.*) Allied to *Euphorbia*.

There is a white-*bracted* variety known as *P. pulcherrima*, variety *Albida*.

Native country Mexico.

Introduced by M. Poinsette in 1834, who discovered the plant in 1828.

Description. A half-shrubby, straggling, stove plant, with ovate leaves and large glowing scarlet bracts, spreading like a star, sometimes as much as a foot in diameter, rendering this one of our most showy stove plants for winter decoration. It is extensively grown for Covent Garden Market, both for cut-flowers and in five-inch pots for decoration. The white variety is also handsome, especially by candle-light.

Culture. Summer temperature 60° to 70°, winter 50° to 55°.

Soil, equal parts of sandy peat, leaf-mould, and fibry loam. When the plant has ceased flowering, it should be cut down to within six inches of the soil, and after that kept in rather a cool and dry situation for two months, then re-potted, furnishing a liberal shift, and placed in a warmer temperature, giving a small supply of water till the young shoots have made some progress. As the rich scarlet bracts are placed at the end of each shoot, the more branches there are produced the better display the plant will make; therefore if the shoots are few at first, stop them to cause more to spring up, but do not stop them after the plant has made a considerable growth, for then the purpose will be defeated. As the plant advances in growth, spread out the shoots to give free exposure to the leaves. Tie the shoots to neat straight sticks, and increase the supply of water. Occasionally a watering with weak liquid manure will assist the growth materially. Use the syringe daily to keep down red spider, and give plenty of air in hot weather. The whole intent of this mode of culture is to throw enough strength into the shoots, and thus prevent them from being weak, for then the bracts will be small, and lose much of their showiness. The real flowers are inconspicuous, though very curious.

Propagation. Take, in spring, young shoots cut close to the old wood, and lay them by for a few days, to dry up the juice, then insert in sand, and place them in a gentle bottom heat, shading from sun-light. When rooted, pot off and shade for a short time, after which gradually inure them to bear full exposure to the light; re-pot as soon as the roots reach the side of the pot, and treat as established plants. Cuttings may be struck from the old wood when the plants are cut down after flowering; these should be in lengths of four inches, and laid on a warm shelf, to dry up the wounds before planting; these are more difficult to manage than young shoots a few inches long, grown in spring.

For the present beautiful plant I am indebted to Miss Fellows, Beeston Hill, Nottinghamshire.

MARANTA PARDINA.
XXXII

MARANTA PARDINA.

PLATE XXXII.

Dear friend, love well the flowers! Flowers are the sign
Of Earth's all gentle love, her grace, her youth,
Her endless, matchless, tender gratitude.
When the Sun shines on thee,—why art thou glad?
But when on Earth he smileth, she bursts forth
In beauty like a bride, and gives him back,
In sweet repayment for his warm bright love,
A world of flowers. You may see them born
On any day in April, moist or dry,
As bright as are the Heavens that look on them;
Some are sown like stars upon the greensward; some
As yellow as the sunrise, others red
As Day is when he sets! reflecting thus,
In pretty moods, the bounties of the sky,
Love *all* flowers, then. Be sure that wisdom lies
In every leaf and bloom; o'er hills and dales,
And thymy mountains; sylvan solitude,
Where sweet-voiced sing the long year through;
In every haunt beneath the eternal Sun,
Where Youth or Age sends forth its grateful prayer,
Or thoughtful Meditation deigns to stray.

Native country New Grenada.

Introduced in 1855, by M. Linden, of Brussels.

The present beautiful species is not well known to the ordinary plant cultivators, being as yet only to be found in the more perfect collections.

Description. A handsome deciduous stove perennial, with ovate leaves, from ten to fifteen inches long, and four to six inches wide, of a pale green colour shaded with white, and dark blotches, almost black. The pretty yellow flowers, of a considerable size, rising well up above the foliage, are the most showy of any species of *Maranta*.

Culture. Summer heat 65° to 75°, winter 55° to 60°. The best soil is leaf-mould, fibrous sandy loam, and peat in equal parts, with a few pieces of charcoal to keep it open; mix all thoroughly, but do not sift the compost. Pot in March; if the plant is in a healthy growing state, give plenty of pot-room, only take care to drain well; nothing is more injurious to these feeding-rooted plants than stagnant water. When the plants are fresh potted, it would help fresh growth amazingly if the pots were plunged in bottom heat, (a tan-bed, or bed of leaves.) Water moderately at first, but more freely as soon as the plants have made new roots, and are commencing to grow freely. If large plants are desired, then re-pot again in June. Let the air of the house be kept moist during the growing season by syringing the pipes, walls, and floor frequently, as the plant is subject to red spider. The plants should go to rest every winter; but if watered and kept in strong heat, they may be kept up all the winter, although they never make such fine plants as when rested a short period, and have not such a healthy foliage. They ought to rest from December to March.

Propagation. By suckers; these are produced freely, and when rooted should be detached from the parent plant by a sharp knife, passing through the connecting rhizoma, and lifting up the young rooted sucker. Pot in a proportionate-sized pot, and either plunge in heat, or place it on a heated surface; keep moist in either case, and covered with a hand-glass till fresh roots and new growth are emitted, then harden off gradually, re-pot, and treat them like the parent.

I am indebted to Messrs. Veitch, of the Exotic Nursery, Chelsea, for leaves of this plant.

GESNERA CINNABARINA.

PLATE XXXIII.

> Then comes the tulip race, where Beauty plays
> Her idle freaks; from family diffus'd
> To family, as flies the father-dust,
> The varied colours run; and, while they break
> On the charm'd eye, th' exulting florist marks,
> With secret pride, the wonders of his hand.
> No gradual bloom is wanting; from the bud,
> First-born of Spring, to Summer's musky tribes:
> Nor hyacinths, of purest virgin white,
> Low-bent, and blushing inward; nor jonquilles,
> Of potent fragrance; nor narcissus fair,
> As o'er the fabled fountain hanging still;
> Nor broad carnations, nor gay-spotted pinks;
> Nor, shower'd from every bush, the damask rose.
> Infinite numbers, delicacies, smells,
> With hues on hues expression cannot paint,
> The breath of Nature, and her endless bloom.
> — THOMSON.

GESNERA, named after the celebrated botanist, Conrad Gesner, of Zurich. Natural order Gesnerworts, *(Gesneraceæ.)* Linnæus, 14.—*Didynamia*, 2.—*Angiospermia*. Allied to *Gloxinia*.

A most beautiful tribe of plants, most of them having scarlet flowers. Sixty or seventy species and varieties have been introduced into this country.

Native country Mexico.

The present species was introduced by Messrs. E. G. Henderson, of the Wellington Nursery, London, from M. Linden, of Brussels.

Description. A deciduous stove plant, flowering from December to April. The leaves are oval-shaped, of a green colour, and have a velvety appearance, being thickly covered with short crimson hairs, which gives them this rich velvety crimson hue. The stem rises to a foot high, and is clothed with the beautiful foliage, above which rises a spike of orange scarlet handsome flowers. *Gesnera cinnabarina* is a great acquisition to our winter-blooming ornamental plants, and should be in every collection.

Culture. The proper compost for this fine plant consists of fibry loam, sandy peat, and decayed vegetable mould in equal parts. The stems lie down after the plant has ceased blooming, and then it requires a period of rest, therefore water should be withheld, and the plant placed in a rather cool, dry portion of the stove for two or three months. The plant has similar bulbs or scaly roots to the well-known *G. zebrina*.

Propagation. About the end of May remove the plants to the potting-bench, turn the bulbs carefully out of the pots and pick out the scaly tubers; put each in a pot four inches across and well drained, in the above compost; one strong plant will give five or six tubers. If it is desired to increase the stock largely, then divide each bulb into several parts, and put three or four of these divisions into the same sized pots; they will make good plants, but will not flower strongly the following season. The entire bulbs will require re-potting in July, and again in September, and will then flower freely in the winter. Heat required, in summer 75° to 80°, winter 65° to 70°.

For the specimen figured my thanks are due to Mr. E. G. Henderson, of the Wellington Nursery.

FUNKIA SIEBOLDIANA VARIEGATA.
XXXIV

FUNKIA SIEBOLDIANA VARIEGATA.

PLATE XXXIV.

Oh! beautiful flowers, what gems ye be!
  Your colours so bright, or pure as the snow;
It is in your faces reflected we see
  All that is lovely, wherever ye grow.

Beautiful leaves that are striped with gold,
  Spangled with silver, or mottled with white,
Welcome as flowers, for when ye unfold,
  Ye shine forth in day, as stars shine at night.

The sun warms your buds till each bursts in bloom,
  Various in tints—some modest, some bright,—
So graceful in form, or sweet your perfume;
  But the leaves drink pearls from the dews of night.

Then welcome, gay flowers, ye bright flowers of spring,
  Born to delight, and to gladden the eye;
But your leaves! thrice welcome, seeing they bring
  Flowers, that without them would fade and die.
                                                    L.

FUNKIA, a genus of hardy herbaceous perennials from Japan, requiring to be grown in a warm, dry situation. Named by Sprengel after Henry Funk, a German Botanist. Natural order *Liliaceæ*. Allied to *Hemerocallis*.

Funkia Sieboldiana variegata is a handsome plant, introduced from the continent in 1834.

Description. A hardy herbaceous perennial, with sub-cordate leaves, about eight or ten inches long, and three or four wide, beautifully variegated, throwing up a flower-stem twelve inches long. The flowers are of a lilac colour, but not very showy.

Culture. Requires a dry situation, and a deep sandy loam. Its beautiful foliage is better developed if kept in a large pot in a cold pit through the winter, and as soon as the leaves begin to spring removed to a greenhouse, placed close to the glass, taking care not to let them suffer for want of water. The variegation is under this treatment more vivid, and better defined.

Propagation. Readily increased by division of the plant into good-sized parts in autumn.

The illustration is from a specimen kindly furnished by Mr Hancock, of Cheshunt, Hertfordshire.

ANŒCTOCHILUS RUBRO-VENIA.

XXXV

ANŒCTOCHILUS RUBRO-VENIA.

(Goodyera rubro-venia.)

PLATE XXXV.

> So have I often seen a purple flower,
>   Fainting through heat, hang down her drooping head,
> But soon refreshed with a welcome shower,
>   Begin again her lively beauties spread,
>   And with new pride her silken leaves display;
>   And while the sun doth now more gentle play,
> Lay out her swelling bosom to the smiling day.
>   PHINEAS FLETCHER.

NATIVE countries Borneo and Ceylon.

Introduced in 1856, by Messrs. Jackson and Son, Nurserymen, Kingston.

Description. An evergreen herbaceous stove plant. Leaves, when full-grown, two inches and a half long, one inch and a half broad; oval-shaped and pointed, with a distinct reddish crimson vein down the centre, and one on each side, curving towards the margin, and meeting the centre one near the apex. The ground colour a rich dark velvety green. Another beautiful addition to this charming genus of beautiful foliaged plants, exceedingly distinct from any other species.

Culture. Pot the plant in a compost of fibry peat and chopped sphagnum in equal parts, adding a small addition of silver-sand and small pieces of charcoal, well mingled with the peat and moss. Fill the pot nearly half full of broken pots, the large pieces at the bottom and smaller at the top. Pot in March, and give but little water at first, until the plant begins to grow, then give more, and as the summer advances cover the plant with a bell-glass, and in very hot weather tilt it on one side to give air. To make a good specimen lay the plant down, and when the stem has grown an inch, and made roots, then cut the prostrate stem in two, leaving roots to the top part: the lower part will soon push forth a fresh top; and this process may be repeated till the plant, or rather plants, fill the entire surface of the pot.

Summer heat 70° to 85°, winter 60° to 65°.

Propagation. This plant, like all its congeners, is increased by dividing the plants into as many parts as there are shoots, with a root to each of them. It is more easy to increase than many others of this genus, though it is as yet extremely rare.

PANDANUS JAVANICUS VARIEGATUS.
XXXVI

PANDANUS JAVANICUS VARIEGATUS.

THE VARIEGATED JAPAN SCREWPINE.

PLATE XXXVI.

> I heard a thousand blended notes,
>   While in a grove I sate reclined,
> In that sweet mood when pleasant thoughts
>   Bring sad thoughts to the mind.
> Through primrose tufts in that green bower
>   The periwinkle trailed its wreaths;
> And 't is my faith that every flower
>   Enjoys the air it breathes.
> The budding twigs spread out their fan
>   To catch the breezy air;
> And I must think, do all I can,
>   That there was pleasure there.
>   WORDSWORTH.

This is a stately fine-looking genus, chiefly from the East Indies, taking its name from a Malay word—*pandang*, signifying conspicuous. Linnæus, 22.—*Diœcia*, 1.—*Monandria*. Natural order Screwpines, *(Pandanaceæ.)*

Stove evergreens, with white flowers. Amongst the most conspicuous may be mentioned—

Pandanus candelabrum, from Guinea, (the Candlestick Screwpine,) which grows to the height of sixty feet.

P. amaryllifolius, (Amaryllis-leaved,) from the East Indies.

P. fascicularis, (fascicled,) from the East Indies.

P. odoratissimus, (sweetest scented,) from the East Indies.

P. spiralis, (spiral,) from New South Wales.

P. utilis, (useful,) Isle of Bourbon. All the last five species attain the height of twenty feet.

However we have only to treat of the beautiful leaved species, *Pandanus javanicus variegatus*.

Native countries Japan and the East Indies.

Introduced about 1842.

Description. A handsome striped-leaved plant, with something like the appearance of a coarse variegated pine-apple, the leaves averaging from two feet six inches to three feet in length, and one inch and a quarter broad, curved, and having the margin serrulated rather thickly with strong spines. The habit is good, for the plant forms a dense bush. The variegation is distinct, the bright colouring of the stripe being clear white, on a dark green ground.

Propagation. By suckers or side-shoots, which are thrown up freely towards the bottom of the stem. Cut one or more off, close to the stem, and remove the lower leaves. Prepare a cutting-pot by well draining and filling it with pure sandy loam. Plant the sucker or side-shoot, and then plunge it in bottom-heat. If a handlight is placed over it roots will be more rapidly emitted. Shade at first from bright sun, and as soon as the roots appear, give less shade, and gradually inure the plants to bear the full sun and air. As soon as the pot is filled with roots re-pot into a rich compost, consisting of fibry loam, sandy peat, and cow dung, with a liberal sprinkling of silver-sand, adding a few bits of charcoal, and plunge in heat. Syringe freely in warm weather, and keep the soil rather moist, and the plant will grow quickly. These plants may be re-potted again the same year, into a considerably larger-sized pot. Continue to keep a moist atmosphere, and a liberal supply of water at the roots. In the following year under this treatment the plant ought to be a considerable size, fit for the exhibition tent.

Summer temperature 60° to 80°, winter 55° to 60°.

For a plant my thanks are due to Messrs. Rollisson, of Tooting.

PTERIS ARGYRÆA.

THE SILVER BRAKE FERN.

PLATE XXXVII.

> Thou hast not left
> Our purer nature, with its fine desires,
> Uncared for in this universe of Thine!
> The glowing rose attests it, the beloved
> Of Poet hearts, touched by their fervent dreams
> With spiritual light, and made a source
> Of heaven-ascending thoughts. The old man's eye
> Falls on the kindling blossoms, and his soul
> Remembers youth and love, and hopefully
> Turns unto Thee, who call'st earth's buried germs
> From dust to splendour; as the mortal seed
> Shall, at Thy summons, from the grave spring up
> To put on glory, to be girt with power,
> And fill'd with immortality. Receive
> Thanks, blessings, love, for these Thy lavish boons,
> And, most of all, their heavenward influences,
> O Thou that gavest us flowers!
> — Mrs. Hemans.

LINNÆUS, 24. Order 1. Natural order *Polypodiaceæ*. An ornamental genus of ferns, taking their name from the Greek *Pteryx*—a wing, in allusion to the form of the fronds. There are stove, greenhouse, and hardy species, and of the latter, *Pteris aquilina*, (or common Brake,) is a well-known and widely-spread British plant. There are nearly forty species at the present time cultivated in this country.

Native country East Indies.

Introduced, in 1858, by Messrs. J. Veitch and Son, of the Royal Exotic Nursery, King's Road, Chelsea.

Description. This is the first variegated fern which has been introduced into this country. It is of free growth, and of good habit, rising three feet high, and spreading its beautiful fronds in the most elegant manner. The pinnæ or side leaves on every frond have a broad central stripe of silvery shining white down the centre, margined with light green, giving it a most charming appearance. No collection of Exotic Ferns should be without this lovely species.

Culture. Summer temperature 70° to 80°, winter 60° to 65°. Requires a compost of sandy peat and leaf-mould in equal parts. Re-pot in March, drain well, and if the plant is in good condition, give a liberal shift. If a few pieces of charcoal are mixed among the compost the plant will thrive all the better. Keep the plant in a rather shady part of the stove, and the fronds will be more distinctly striped.

Propagation. By division; when a plant has two or three crowns, one may be divided off, taking care to preserve all the roots belonging to it. Pot the division in the above compost, and shade densely for a week or two, then remove the shade by degrees until the plant will bear the full light in a fernery or stove.

The illustration is from a frond sent by Mr. E. Cooling, Nurseryman, of Derby.

MARANTA VITTATA
XXXVIII

MARANTA VITTATA.

THE RIBBONED MARANTA.

PLATE XXXVIII.

> The soft sweet moss shall be thy bed,
> With crawling woodbine overspread,
> By which the silver-shedding streams
> Shall gently melt thee into dreams.
> Thy clothing neat shall be a gown
> Made of the fleece's purest down.
> The tongues of kids shall be thy meat,
> Their milk thy drink, and thou shalt eat
> The paste of filberts for thy bread,
> With cream of cowslips buttered.
> Thy feasting tables shall be hills,
> With daisies spread and daffodils,
> Where thou shalt sit, and redbreast by
> For meat shall give thee melody.
> I'll give thee chains and carconets
> Of primroses and violets.
> — HERRICK.

For full particulars of the genus *Maranta* refer to other species already described.

Native country South America.

Introduced into Europe by M. Linden, of the Royal Botanic and Zoological Gardens, Brussels.

Description. A handsome, perennial, evergreen, stove plant, with long oval leaves tapering to a point, and barred in an angular direction, with silvery white stripes on each side the nerves. It is one of the handsomest plants of the genus, because the variegation is perfect all the year.

Culture. Summer temperature 65° to 70°, winter 55° to 60°. Requires a rich compost, consisting of fibrous loam two parts, sandy peat one part, rotten dung and leaf-mould one part, the whole liberally intermixed with silver-sand, to which must be added a few small pieces of charcoal. In summer water freely, in winter very sparingly. Re-pot in March, and if convenient, plunge in a warm tan or leaf bed. Grown in the pine stove this plant thrives well.

Propagation. The plant sends out side-shoots or off-sets, and when these have put out roots of their own, they may be cut off with a sharp knife, and lifted out with the same instrument, and potted in the above compost. Plunge in bottom heat, and place a bell or hand-glass over them until they are rooted, then gradually inure to bear the full light, re-pot, and afterwards treat as established plants.

The illustration is from a specimen kindly furnished by Messrs. J. Veitch and Son, Exotic Nursery, Chelsea.

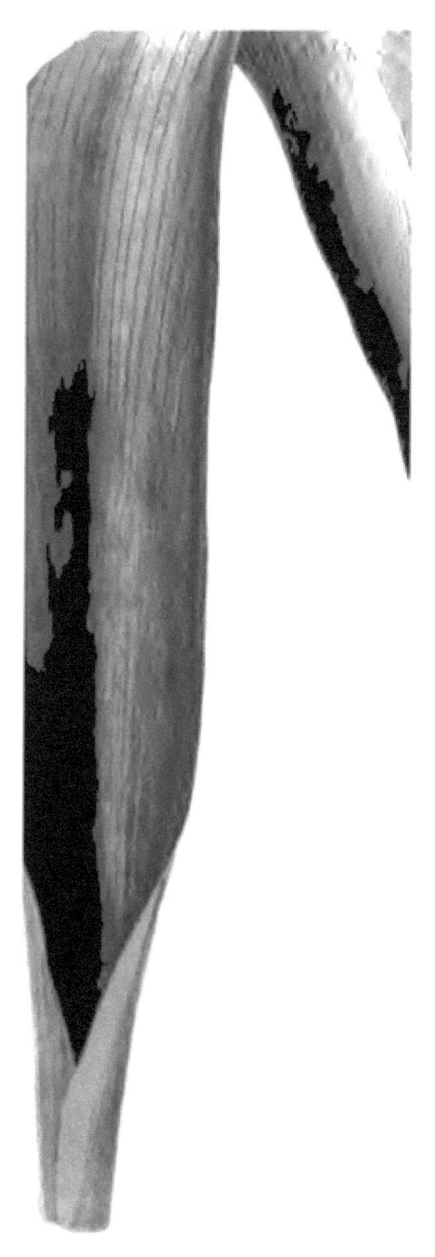

TRADESCANTIA ODORATISSIMA
XXXIX

TRADESCANTIA ODORATISSIMA.

PLATE XXXIX.

> The lily is lovely as when it slept
> On the waters of Eden's lake;
> The woodbine breathes sweetly as when it crept
> In Eden, from brake to brake.
> They were left as a proof of loveliness
> Of Adam and Eve's first home;
> They are here as a type of the joys that bless
> The just in the world to come.
>   The bright, bright flowers!

TRADESCANTIA, Linnæus, named after John Trandescant, gardener to King Charles the First. The tomb of this gardener, which was becoming defaced by age, has, through the instrumentality of Dr. Forbes Young, (a patron of Botany,) been restored. This is the more interesting, as it is a desirable work of art, independently of being the reminder of one of our earliest English gardeners.

Linnæus, 6.—*Hexandria*, 1.—*Monogynia*. Natural order *Spiderworts, (Commelinaceæ.)*

An interesting tribe of plants, consisting of hardy annuals, greenhouse herbaceous, stove herbaceous, and hardy herbaceous species. The hardy ones are from Texas and North America, the greenhouse ones from Mexico, and the stove species from Jamaica, Brazil, South America, Trinidad, East Indies, and Peru. Most of the species have blue flowers.

The present plant was found in the stove at Messrs. Veitch and Sons' Nursery, Chelsea. No record kept as to its native country, nor when introduced.

Description. A most distinct and striking fine-foliaged stove plant. The younger leaves are of a bright green colour, changing to a deep rich purple; and its flowers, which are numerous, produced on a spike about six inches long, are of a beautiful clear blue colour; altogether it is a most ornamental plant, either in or out of flower, and one which, from its high decorative character, should be in every collection.

Culture. Summer heat 70° to 75°, winter 60° to 65°. Soil fibrous loam, fibrous sandy peat, and decayed leaf-mould in equal parts, freely mixed with silver-sand. Drain well, and give liberal pottings. The plants with this treatment will grow fast, and make a fine appearance.

Propagation. Increased by suckers, which are produced plentifully at the base of the plant. Take one or more off, if with roots so much the better, pot them in small pots, with a thin layer of white sand on the surface; give a gentle watering, and place them under a handlight, either on a warm tan-bed or on a heated surface of moist sand; keep them in this situation till fresh roots are emitted, then give air gradually, and inure by degrees to bear full exposure. Then re-pot, and afterwards treat them the same as the established plants.

The illustration is from a plant of Messrs. Veitch and Son, Exotic Nursery, Chelsea.

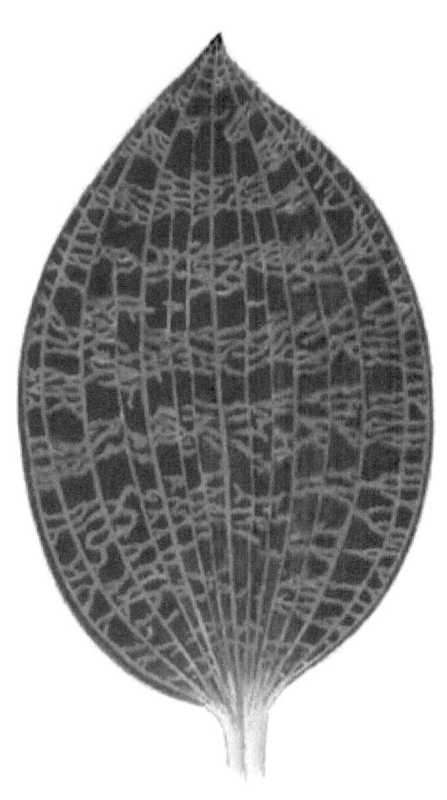

ANOECTOCHILUS LOWII.
XL

ANŒCTOCHILUS LOWII.

PLATE XL.

> They come with genial airs and skies,
>   In summer's golden prime,
> And to the stricken world give back
>   Lost Eden's blissful clime.
> Out-shining Solomon they come,
>   And go full soon away.
> But yet, like him, they meekly breathe
>   True wisdom while they stay.
> 'If God,' they whisper, 'smiles on us,
>   And bids us bloom and shine,
> Does he not mark, oh, faithless man!
>   Each wish and want of thine?'
>
> LYONS.

For an account of this genus see page 13.

Native country Borneo. Introduced in 1852, by Messrs. Low and Son, of Clapton, near London.

Description. This species is the most easy to cultivate of any of the tribe. It is of a more strong and robust habit, hence it is not so liable to damp off in winter. The leaves of a fine plant are fully four inches long and two inches and a half wide. Their ground-colour is of a rich dark velvety green, rather faintly striped and veined with a metallic red.

Culture. Requires a temperature of from 75° to 80° in summer, and from 65° to 70° in winter. This plant grows most freely in chopped sphagnum moss, mixed with some very fibry peat, pieces of charcoal, and a sprinkling of silver-sand. It should be kept under a bell-glass, or in a small frame inside the stove, set on a heated surface of moist sand.

It sends out side-shoots, which may be taken off when

rooted, potted in the above compost, and treated similarly to established plants, only keeping them more densely shaded till fresh growth has taken place. All this tribe thrives best in a close moist atmosphere.

The illustration is from a plant supplied by Mr. Howard.

CROTON VARIEGATUM ANGUSTIFOLIUM
XLI

CROTON VARIEGATUM ANGUSTIFOLIUM.

PLATE XLI.

> "A THING of beauty is a joy for ever:
> Its loveliness increases; it will never
> Pass into nothingness; but still will keep
> A bower of quiet for us, and a sleep
> Full of sweet dreams, and health, and quiet breathing.
> Therefore on every morrow are we wreathing
> A flowery band to bind us to the earth,
> Spite of despondence, of the inhuman dearth
> Of noble natures, of the gloomy days,
> Of all the unhealthy and o'er-darken'd ways
> Made for our searching: yea, in spite of all,
> Some shape of beauty moves away the pall
> From our dark spirits. Such is the sun, the moon,
> Trees old and young, sprouting a shady boon
> For simple sheep; and such are daffodils,
> With the green world they live in, and clear rills
> That for themselves a cooling covert make
> 'Gainst the hot season; the mid-forest brake,
> Rich with a sprinkling of fair musk-rose blooms;
> An endless fountain of immortal drink,
> Pouring unto us from the heaven's brink."
>
> KEATS.

THIS genus is described at page 4.

The present species is a native of India, and was introduced in 1847.

Description. A stove evergreen shrub, with inconspicuous white and green flowers. The leaves are from a foot to eighteen inches long, and three quarters of an inch broad; they droop gracefully downward, and are beautifully striped with yellow on either side of the midrib of each leaf. The stem is stout, erect, and but rarely branches. A good specimen of it well grown is a handsome object.

Culture. Requires a warm stove. Summer heat 75° to 80°, winter heat 65° to 70°. Soil—sandy fibrous peat and turfy loam in equal parts, with a liberal addition of silver-sand, will grow it well. No stimulating agents, such as rotten dung, leaf-mould, or liquid manure, should be used, for this will cause the variegation to be less dense.

Propagation. About the end of July, just as the summer shoots are beginning to harden, take them off at the point between this and the last year's wood; smooth the bottom of each cutting with a sharp knife, and cut off the lower leaves close to the bark without injuring it. The leaves that are left should be cut to about half their length. Insert the cuttings in a pot, well drained and filled with the compost to about an inch of the rim, and the rest with silver-sand. Water well to set the sand close to the cuttings; then place them under a bell-glass, taking care to prop up the leaves, so that they do not touch the bell-glass. Plunge the pot in heat, shade from the sun, and give water as it is required. In six weeks time they should be rooted, when it is requisite to move them into small pots, and re-place them under a close glass, and as soon as fresh roots are emitted re-pot again, and gradually harden them to bear the full light. After this give water moderately, and afterwards treat them as established plants, stopping occasionally to cause the plant to become bushy.

For a plant my thanks are due to Messrs. Jackson, of Kingston.

CONVALLARIA MAJALIS VARIEGATA.
XLII

CONVALLARIA MAJALIS VARIEGATA.

PLATE XLII.

> Deep solitude I sought. There was a dell
> Where woven shades shut out the eye of day,
> While, towering near, the rugged mountains made
> Dark back-ground 'gainst the sky. Thither I went,
> And bade my spirit drink that lonely draught,
> For which it long had languish'd mid the strife
> And fever of the world. I thought to be
> There without witness. But the violet's eye
> Look'd up upon me,—the fresh wild-rose smiled,
> And the young pendant vine-flower kiss'd my cheek.
> And there were voices too. The garrulous brook
> Untiring to the patient pebbles told
> Its history;—up came the singing breeze,
> And the broad leaves of the cool poplar spake
> Responsive every one. Trees, flowers, and streams,
> Are social and benevolent; and he
> Who oft communeth in their language pure,
> Roaming among them at the cool of day,
> Shall find, like him who Eden's garden dress'd,
> His maker there, to teach his listening heart.
> Sigourney.

Convallaria, Linnæus, is from the Latin *Convallis*, a valley, in allusion to the situation where it grows, hence the English name "Lily of the Valley." Linnæus, 6; order 1; natural order *Liliaceæ*. A native of Great Britain. Within a short walk of Matlock there are many acres of land entirely covered with the *Convallaria majalis*, which, when in bloom, is worthy of a long journey to see, and whose perfume scents the air for a great distance.*

A garden variety.

Description. A perennial herbaceous plant, with oval-shaped leaves; each leaf beautifully striped longitudinally with golden-coloured lines running from the base to the apex; variegation constant.

---

* This lovely place is known as the *Via Gellia*.

The flowers are well known for their humble beauty and delicious fragrance.

Culture. The present variety should be grown in rather a poor sandy loam, and in a shady place, although it will also succeed on a south border. To obtain a good plant with clear golden stripes, it is recommended to be grown in a pot, and during the infoliation kept in a cold pit or frame. Rain and wind are injurious elements to any fine-foliaged plant. Towards the autumn, as soon as the leaves begin to fade, plunge the pots containing these plants in an open border. In February or March remove the surface soil, and give a top-dressing of fresh loam. Take care that there are no worms in the pot, and that the drainage is good.

Propagation. It is a plant that is very easy of propagation. When it is desirable to increase the stock, the plants may be taken up in February and March, cut into small pieces about two inches long, and the creeping roots planted in an open border six inches apart, and these in the course of a year will make good plants.

The illustration is from a plant kindly furnished by Mr. George Paul, Cheshunt, Herts.

CALADIUM PICTUM.

PLATE XLIII.

> There is beauty o'er all this delectable world,
> Which wakes at the first golden touch of the light;
> There is beauty when morn hath her banner unfurl'd,
> Or when stars twinkle out from the depths of the night.
> There is beauty on ocean's vast verdureless plains,
> Though lashed into fury or lull'd into calm;
> There is beauty on land, and its countless domains—
> Its corn-fields of plenty—its meadows of balm;—
> Oh, God of Creation! these sights are of Thee!
> Thou surely hast made them for all that are free!
> — Prince.

For a description of this genus see page 7.

Native country Rio.

Introduced about 1850, from the Continent.

Description. A handsome tuberous-rooted, herbaceous, stove perennial. Leaf-stems about eighteen inches high, and of a rich purple colour. Leaves heart-shaped, about a foot long and seven inches broad, irregularly blotched with white spots on a light green ground. A fine plant kept in a stove or orchid house keeps its foliage all the year with a little care in watering.

Culture. Summer heat 70° to 80°, winter 65° to 70°. Soil lumpy turf, sandy peat, and dried cow-dung in equal parts, mixed with silver-sand, will grow it well. Re-pot in March, using a somewhat large-sized pot, taking care to drain well. Water freely during the summer, using liquid manure often; water sparingly in winter. Take care that no worms are in the pot, and keep the plant near the glass. In case the green fly makes its appearance, at once apply tobacco water in a diluted state, or give a gentle smoking; if this pest remains on the young foliage, it will cause it to become deformed and wrinkled.

Propagation. By division of the roots and young suckers, which spring up from the parent rootstock, and by division of the roots in spring, cut in small pieces wherever there is a crown. Pot the suckers, and place them under a close frame for a week or ten days, until they are established.

A handsome desirable plant, either for decoration or exhibition.

My thanks are due to Messrs. Jackson, of Kingston, for plants of this species, and to Mr. Veitch for leaves.

XLIV

HOYA CARNOSA FOLIIS VARIEGATA.

THE VARIEGATED-LEAVED HOYA.

PLATE XLIV.

The bloom is on the cherry-tree, the leaf is on the elm,
The bird and butterfly have come to claim their fairy realm;
Unnumbered stars are on the earth, the fairest who can choose,
When all are painted with the tints that form the rainbow hues?
What spirit-wand hath wakened them?—the branch of late was bare,
The world was desolate, but now there's beauty everywhere.
Yes, the sweet and merry sunshine has unfolded leaf and flower,
To tell us of the Infinite, of Glory, and of Power.

ELIZA COOK.

NATURAL order Asclepiads, *(Asclepiadaceæ,)* Linnæus, 5.—*Pentandria*, 2.—*Digynia.*

Native country Asia.

Introduced from the Ghent Nurseries in 1850.

The genus *Hoya* was named in honour of Thomas Hoy. The various species bear remarkably handsome flowers, very waxy in appearance, especially *H. bella* and *H. imperialis;* however, the present book being devoted to "Beautiful Leaved Plants," our description is confined to those whose leaves are variegated.

Description. Leaves thick and fleshy, oval-shaped, about three inches long by an inch and a half wide, and richly variegated. A climbing evergreen stove plant of considerable beauty. Its flowers are in drooping umbels, each flower producing a drop of pure honey; hence it has been called the Honey Plant. This variety produces the same kind of flowers as *Hoya carnosa*, but not so freely, which may be owing to its requiring age before it flowers.

Culture. Summer temperature 65° to 70°, winter 50° to 55°. This plant requires a poor open soil: the best compost for it consists of loam, peat, and little pieces of broken pots or bricks and old lime rubbish in equal parts, well mixed together. The plant should be kept rather under-potted, in order to keep its variegation more distinct. The season for re-potting is early spring. Take the plant to the potting-bench, turn it carefully out, then pick out the old drainage and as much of the old soil as can be taken away without injuring the roots of the plant. Drain the fresh pot well, cover the drainage with a layer of moss or rough peat, place the ball in the centre, cover it with the new compost till the pot is full, then give a smart stroke or two on the bench, to settle the soil firmly about the plant. Give no water for a week or two, till fresh roots are produced, then a gentle watering, and increase the quantity as the plant grows and the season advances. In the autumn and winter months give water very moderately, if any, for if kept wet the roots must perish.

As this is a climbing plant, and requires training, the best plan is to form a kind of balloon-shaped trellis. Procure a number of neat sticks, painted green, thrust them in the pot at equal distances, close to the side, then place a stout wire ring rather wider in diameter than the pot, about half-way between the rim of the pot and the top of the sticks. Tie each stick to the ring, then bring their tops together, and tie them securely. Draw the shoots of the plant through the sticks, and train them at equal distances round the trellis. When the trellis is covered with shoots and leaves it forms a very handsome object.

Propagation. By cuttings and leaves. Take them off, and lay them on a shelf for a day or two, to heal up the wounds and stop the bleeding. Then put them round the sides of the pot, well drained, and plunge the pot in a moist heat, giving but little water till roots are emitted. It strikes very easily and quickly. When sufficient roots are emitted, pot them off separately, placing them again in a moist heat, until they are established, then treat as the parent plant.

GRAPTOPHYLLUM PICTUM
XLV

GRAPTOPHYLLUM PICTUM, OR ALBUM.

PLATE XLV.

> AND what is so rare as a day in June?
> Then, if ever, come perfect days;
> Then heaven tries the earth if it be in tune,
> And over it softly her warm ear lays:
> Whether we look, or whether we listen,
> We hear life murmur, or see it glisten;
> Every clod feels a stir of might,
> An instinct within it that reaches and towers,
> And, grasping blindly above it for light,
> Climbs to a soul in grass and flowers;
> The flush of life may well be seen,
> Thrilling back over hills and valleys;
> The cowslip startles in meadows green,
> The buttercup catches the sun in its chalice,
> And there's never a leaf or blade too mean
> To be some happy creature's palace.
>
> LOWELL.

NATURAL order Acanthads, *(Acanthaceæ.)* Linnæus, 2.—*Diandria*, 1.—*Monogynia*, allied to *Beloperone*.

Native country East Indies. Introduced in 1815.

Description. A shrubby stove plant, growing from eight to ten feet high, with smooth green leaves, blotched irregularly with pale yellow and white blotches, which are said to represent the human face if the likeness can be found out. It is, however, a beautiful variegated shrub. Like *Croton variegatum*, it should be fully exposed to the sun to bring out the full variegation, as if grown in the shade the colours are faint and ill-defined.

Culture. Summer heat 65° to 75°, winter 50° to 55°. Strong fibry loam, sandy peat, and well-decomposed dung, is the right compost. It should be rather under-potted, to keep down the luxuriant growth. The plant is apt to grow straggling, hence it should be pruned in and stopped freely, and this will induce a bushy habit. So managed it forms a striking object in a short time.

Propagation. Young tops taken off at a joint and planted in silver-sand under a handlight or bell-glass, strike very freely. As soon as roots are emitted, pot them off, immediately replace them, and shade for a few days, then gradually inure them to bear full exposure.

The specimen for illustration was kindly furnished by Mr. Veitch, Royal Exotic Nursery, Chelsea.

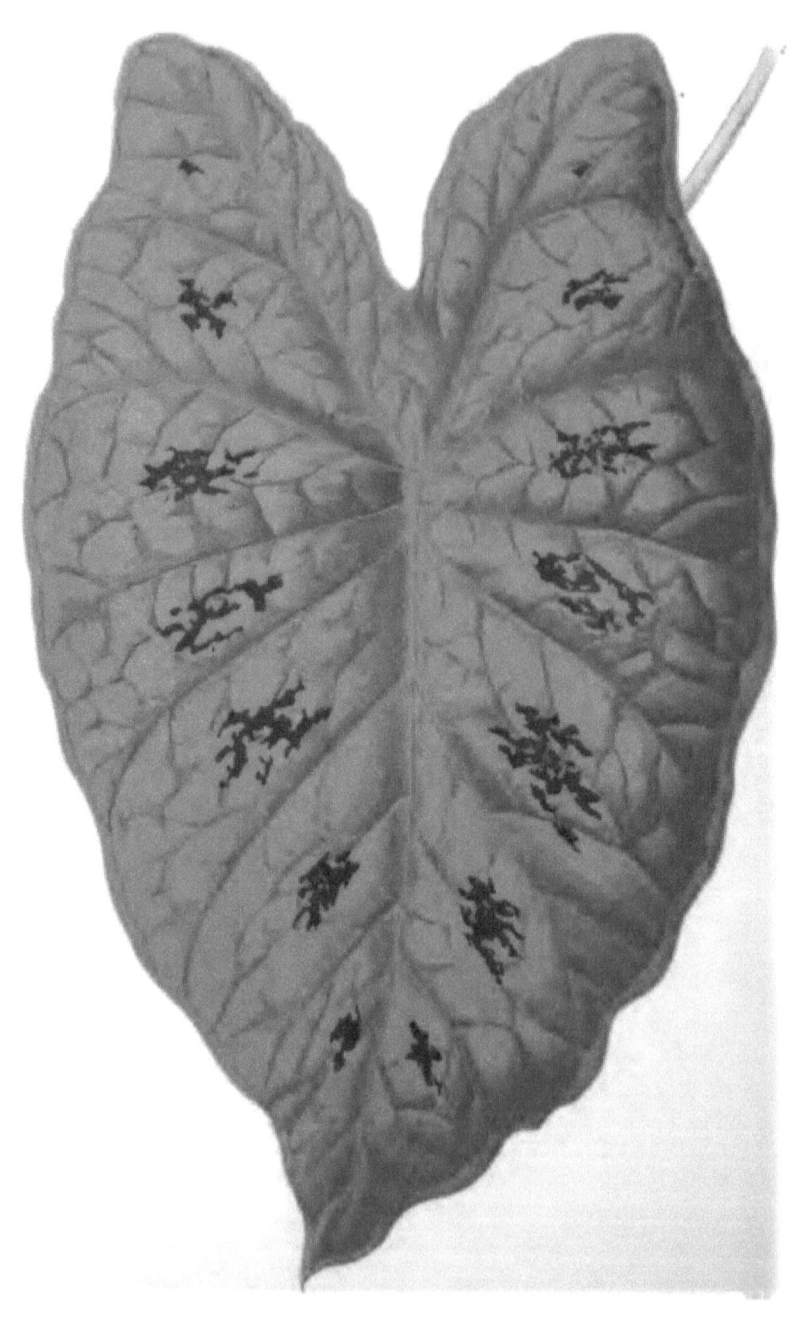

CALADIUM VERSCHAFFELTI.
XLVI

CALADIUM VERSCHAFFELTI.

PLATE XLVI.

> See, the many-coloured train,
> Peeping upon glade and plain—
> Crocuses, and snowdrops white,
> Struggle into sunny light,
> And the violet of blue,
> And the valley's lily too.
> I could dream their fairy bells
> Ring a merry chime, that tells
> Spring is coming!—and when they
> Faint, and fade, and fall away,
> 'Tis that long by winter nurst,
> Their full hearts with joy have burst.
> CAMILLA TOULMIN.

For a description of the genus, see page 7.

Native country the banks of the Amazon River, South America.

Introduced by M. Chantin, of Paris, in 1857.

Description. This plant usually attains the height of two feet. The leaves are heart-shaped, six to nine inches long, and four inches wide; the ground colour brilliant green, with bright red spots placed irregularly in the leaf. A distinct and beautiful species, well worthy of a situation in the choicest collection of beautiful foliaged plants.

Culture. Summer temperature 70° to 80°, winter 60° to 65°.

Soil. Turfy loam, sandy peat, and decayed dung, in equal parts, with a few pieces of charcoal mixed throughout the whole. Like most of its congeners, in winter it should have a short cessation from growth, and kept tolerably, but not particularly, dry. In early spring, as soon as growth begins, the plants ought to be re-potted. Shake them out of the old soil, and re-pot in fresh compost, and give but very little water until the plant has made a good start, then re-pot, and if convenient, plunge in a little bottom-heat, and increase both top-heat and moisture. The plants will grow rapidly, and will require a third potting about the end of June. Give plenty of water in summer, and occasionally liquid manure. By the middle of August the plant will be in splendid perfection.

Propagation. Like the rest of the genus, this species sends forth side-shoots, which, when rooted, may be taken off, potted, and placed in a gentle bottom-heat under a bell-glass or frame for a few days, and well shaded. They soon make growth, if care is taken not to expose them too quickly: treat as parent plants, continuing to re-pot as the roots get to the pot sides.

Mr. J. Veitch, of the Exotic Nursery, Chelsea, kindly favoured us with the specimen for our illustration.

PTERIS ASPERICAULIS.
Var. Tricolor.

PTERIS ASPERICAULIS, Var. Tricolor.

PLATE XLVII.

"Go, form a monitory wreath
　For youth's unthinking brow,
Go, and to busy manhood breathe
　What most he fears to know;
Go, strew the path where age doth tread,
And tell him of the silent dead.
Go, then, where, wrapt in fear and gloom,
　Fond hearts and true are sighing,
And wreathe with emblematic bloom,
　The pillow of the dying;
And say, that He who from the dust
　Recalls the slumbering flower,
Will surely visit those who trust
　His mercy and his power,—
Will mark where sleeps their peaceful clay,
And roll, ere long, the stone away!"

For a description of this genus see *Pteris argyrea*, page 75. A most beautiful fern. Native country South America.

Introduced in 1857, by Mr. Linden, of the Royal Botanic and Zoological Gardens, Brussels.

Description. A tall-growing beautiful Fern, with the fronds bipinnate; pinnæ striped down the centre on each side of the main rib (which is of a rich crimson hue) with white. Certainly the most distinct variegated fern yet introduced.

Culture. Requires the heat of the stove, and to be grown in a shady place in summer. Rough sandy peat and half-decayed leaves in equal parts, with a sprinkling of silver-sand; the pots to be well drained. It should be re-potted in March, and again in June, for if the pots become too full of roots the plants will not thrive well, nor put forth fine fronds. It is requisite to keep the plant constantly well watered, for if the soil becomes quite dry the plant will perish.

Propagation. As it is not yet known whether this plant will come true from spores, it must therefore be propagated by division of the roots. When the plant becomes large it will send forth side-shoots. As soon as these side-shoots have roots of their own, divide them from the parent plant, and pot them in the compost, in proportionate-sized pots, and place them under a bell-glass or propagating frame till a fresh growth is perceived, then gradually inure to bear the full light, and afterwards treat them the same as the parent plant.

The illustration is from a plant forwarded by Mr. E. Cooling, Mile-ash Nursery, Derby.

CRATAEGUS PRUNIFOLIA VARIEGATA.
XLVIII

CRATÆGUS PRUNIFOLIA VARIEGATA.

THE GOLDEN VARIEGATED THORN.

PLATE XLVIII.

> WHAT is beauty? Come with me
> Into Nature's sanctuary;
> To the mead or the wild-wood,
> Where the flowers, in blooming childhood,
> From the emerald sod look up.
> Each has a diamond in its cup,
> A silver or a golden cell,
> Where a fairy queen might dwell.
> Come where the yellow broom is waving,
> Or the stream the lily laving;
> Where the hawthorn scents the gale,
> And zephyr, wandering through the vale,
> Bears on its aërial wing
> The breath of each odorous thing;
> Where plumy fern, of brightest green,
> And moss of every hue is seen;
> There doth Nature's self control
> Each emotion of the soul;
> Make thy heart with joy confess,
> If there's beauty, it is this!
>
> J. C.

THE name *Cratægus* is derived from *Kratos*, signifying strength, in allusion to the hardness of the wood. This very ornamental genus is composed of hardy trees and shrubs, many species being native of North America.—Linn. 12, Ord. 2. Most of them bear white blossoms, the flowers being much admired, for who does not admire even our common hawthorn, (*Cratægus oxycantha*,) and its lovely varieties,—*punicea*, scarlet-flowered, *puniceum flore-pleno*, double scarlet-flowered, *rosea superba*, crimson, *plena*, double white, *aurea*, golden-berried, *leucocarpa*, white-fruited, *oliveriana*, black-berried, or *quercifolia*, oak-leaved.

There is a peculiar interest attached to the hawthorn; it is one of our first shrubs to come into leaf in early spring, whilst its blossom seems to tell us of the arrival of warm weather.

In England, being so much used as the boundary to fields, roads, and railways, it is constantly before our eyes; we see it in all its different aspects, freshly green when most other trees are leafless, and anon covered with its scented white blossoms, or in winter denuded of leaves, yet scarlet with innumerable berries, the favourite food of our winter migratory birds, the Fieldfare and the Redwing.* However, returning to our subject, the variegated variety of *Cratægus prunifolia* deserves our attention.

Raised from seed by Mr. Joshua Major, Landscape Gardener, Knosthorpe, near Leeds.

Description. A low bushy tree, with large broadly ovate leaves and spineless branches. The leaves are variegated, and the variegation is rich and constant. This hawthorn is perfectly hardy, and is a great acquisition to our variegated ornamental foliaged trees.

Culture. A common soil, not too rich, will grow this plant well; if too highly manured the leaves might occasionally be green, hence it should be grown in good pure loam, and in a situation fully exposed to the sunlight to bring out its beautiful colours.

Propagation. It may be increased by budding and grafting on the common whitethorn. Bud in June or July, and graft in March. Choose the buds and grafts from such shoots as are bearing and have borne the best-variegated leaves. As soon as the buds or grafts have made some growth rub off all other shoots, and thus give the variegated shoot the full strength of the stock.

The specimen for illustration was kindly furnished by Mr. Joshua Major.

* Whilst alluding to this plant and these birds, I cannot refrain from mentioning what came under my own notice several years ago, a circumstance so remarkable as scarcely to be credited. In my garden there was a large scarlet thorn loaded with berries, which was much frequented by Redwings. One Sunday, soon after my return from church, a flock of these birds alighted on the tree for their accustomed repast. On going into the garden half an hour afterwards, my attention was attracted by a Redwing struggling to get free from something that held it securely; a near inspection shewed me that it was frozen by its tail to the branch. After a sharp hoar frost, a few minutes had thawed the ice into globules of water, which had again become frozen, and one of these globules had sealed a couple of feathers of the bird's tail to a small branch. A pair of scissors quickly cut off the feathers, and after warming the little prisoner by the fire, it was released from captivity, the feathers alone remaining in my possession as trophies to tell of this remarkable *tail* (tale.)

EUONYMUS JAPONICUS AUREUS VARIEGATUS.

GOLDEN-STRIPED JAPAN SPINDLE TREE.

PLATE XLIX.—A.

> "Oh! bring thy couch where countless roses
> The garden's gay retreat discloses;
> There in the shade of waving boughs recline,
> Breathing rich odours, quaffing ruby wine!
> Thou, fairest rose of all, oh! say,
> For whom thy hundred leaves doth thou display?"
> L. S. Costello.

Euonymus is derived from *eu*, good, and *onoma*, a name. Natural order *Celastraceæ*, Linnæus,'5.—*Pentandria*, 1.—*Monogynia*. Interesting hardy and half-hardy shrubs, growing from five to fifteen feet high.

Native country of the present species Japan.

Introduced in its variegated state in 1836.

Description. A low-growing evergreen shrub, not quite hardy in the north of England. Leaves ovate, striped and blotched with gold, on a verdure green ground; about an inch and a half long, by an inch wide. When in its most perfect state it is really a beautiful foliaged plant.

Culture. This plant requires a sandy loam on a dry subsoil, and should be planted in a sheltered place in the south. North of the Trent it should either be planted against a south wall, and trained to it, or should be protected in a cold frame, which implies the taking up of it in autumn, and potting previous to placing it in its winter quarters; keeping the plant in a pot, and plunging it out of doors during the summer months, would bring the foliage better variegated.

Propagation. Increased by cuttings and layers; by layers in June. Choose the best variegated shoots, bring them carefully to the ground, then make a slit on the under side, (similar to laying a carnation,) peg down the shoots, and cover an inch deep with light sandy soil. In the autumn of the following year the layers will be sufficiently rooted to take off the parent plant; pot, and keep in a cold pit until spring, then plant them where they are to remain. Cuttings strike very freely taken from a plant that has been kept under glass. In March select the best variegated shoots, and take off as many cuttings as may be required; trim off all the lower leaves, and place the cuttings in a well-drained pot in silver-sand, give a gentle watering to settle the sand, and plunge in a gentle heat. When these cuttings are rooted pot off singly in four-inch pots, and re-place in heat for a time. This variety may also be increased by grafting on the plain form, for a stock in pots: the season for this is March, and after they are grafted they should be placed on a gentle heat, where they will unite in a few weeks, and may then be hardened off, and treated as the parent plant.

The specimen for illustration was forwarded by Mr. Joshua Major, Landscape Gardener, Knosthorpe, near Leeds.

MARANTA MICANS.

PLATE XLIX.—B.

> "ALL hail, Bokhara, land of flowers!
> Our prince moves proudly on;
> He goes to glad thy sunny bowers,
> He asks thy smile alone.
> The waving cypress seeks his native groves,
> The rising moon the firmament it loves."
> The Rose Garden of Persia, L. S. COSTELLO.

NATIVE country Tropical America. Introduced in 1854.

Description. This is the smallest species in habit of the genus. It is a lovely little gem, having dark green foliage, with a white feathery shining stripe along the centre of each leaf. When well grown, and in perfect health, few plants have a more interesting appearance.

Culture. This genus requires great attention to keep in good health. The soil used should be very fibrous peat, with a few small pieces of charcoal intermixed, and abundance of silver-sand. The pot must be rather small in proportion to the size of the plant, and the drainage always kept in good order by a thin layer of sphagnum moss between it and the soil. The plant should be placed on a shelf near to the glass, but carefully shaded from the sun.

Propagation. Side suckers with roots may be cut off carefully and potted in the proper compost, and placed on moist sand under a hand-light or small frame in the warmest part of the stove. Care should be taken to shade from sunlight till a fresh growth has taken place, after which gradually inure to bear the same treatment as the established plants.

DAPHNE MEZEREUM VARIEGATUM.

DAPHNE MEZEREUM VARIEGATUM.

VARIEGATED MEZEREON.

PLATE I.

> Learn from birds and flowers, oh, man!
> Virtues that may gild thy name;
> And their faults, if thou wouldst scan,
> Know thy failings are the same.
> Azz. Eddin Elmocadessi, translated by L. S. Costello.

Daphne mezereum, although occasionally found wild in England, is not considered to be a British plant. Linnæus named this species from *dais*, to burn, and *phone*, a noise, on account of its crackling when burning. Linnæus 8, order 1, natural order *Thymelaceæ*.

The different species are all handsome shrubs, dwarf in habit, and native of Italy, Austria, Spain, France, Switzerland, Siberia, China, England, Japan, Crete, and Jamaica.

Daphne mezereum blooms before it puts forth its leaves. As a welcome garden plant the *Daphne cneorum*, another species, a native of Austria, is a general favourite.

The present variety was raised from seed by Mr. Joshua Major, Landscape Gardener, Knosthorpe, Leeds. He says, "I first found it in 1856, amongst a quantity of seedlings in my grounds. Some of the branches were striped, others not; but my foreman was very particular in grafting only from variegated branches, consequently all the branches on the worked plants are distinctly striped." Mr. Howard can bear testimony to the truth of the last remark, for when he saw them last summer every leaf was most beautifully and regularly variegated.

Description. Like its parent this variety is a low bushy shrub, with ovate leaves, richly edged with pure white.

Culture. Requires a pure sandy dry loam, without any manure mixed with it at any time. It does not thrive well near a smoky town or in wet soils.

Propagation. By grafting early in March. As the branches are small, the kind of grafting called saddle-grafting is the best for this beautiful plant. The method is first to shape the top of the stock like a wedge; then split the scion quite up the centre, and fit it upon the wedge-like top of the stock, making the bark of the stock and scion come in contact. Tie securely, and cover with grafting-clay or wax. It will not want much more attention until the scion commences growing.

The specimen for illustration was furnished by Mr. Major.

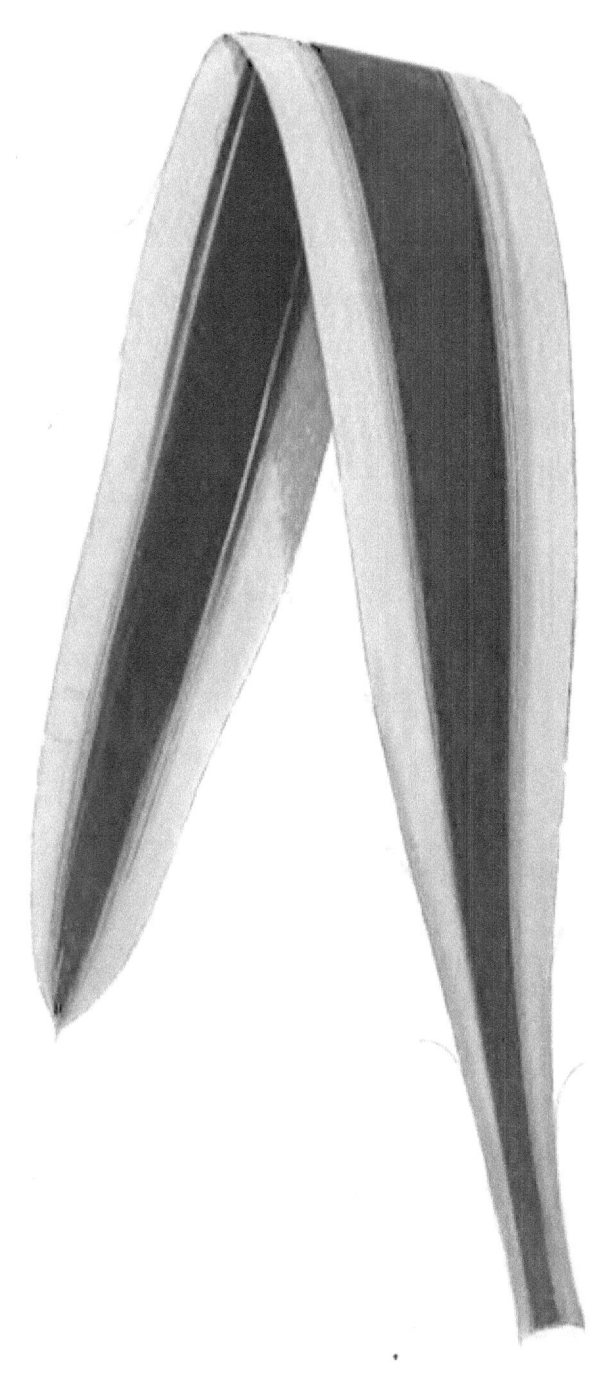

YUCCA FILAMENTOSA VARIEGATA

YUCCA FILAMENTOSA, Var. Variegata.

VARIEGATED THREADY ADAM'S NEEDLE.

PLATE LI.

> "Look forth companions, cast afar your eyes
> Where yonder many-coloured plain extends:
> Ah! in my breast what sweet emotions rise!
> Behold how each soft charm of nature blends
> Into one glorious whole,—grove, mead, or stream,—
> A fit abode for heroes it might seem!
> The tender silken grass invites the tread;
> With musky odour breathes the fanning air;
> Pure waters glide along their perfumed bed,
> As though the rose gave them her essence rare;
> The lily-stalk bends with her fragrant flower,
> The lustre of the rose glads ev'ry bower.
> Oh! never, never,—long as time shall last,—
> May shadows o'er these beauteous scenes be cast!
> Still may they in eternal splendour glow,
> And be like Paradise, as they are now!"
>
> From the Shah Namah of Fendusi.

The genus *Yucca* takes its name from its Peruvian name. Natural order *Liliaceæ*. Linnæus, 6.—*Hexandria*, 1.—*Monogynia*. Exceedingly handsome evergreens, with the habit of palm-trees.

The species, of which a variegated variety is here described, is an especial favourite in gardens; but, although introduced nearly one hundred and fifty years ago, it is comparatively scarce.

Native country Virginia. Introduced about 1720.

Description. A hardy evergreen herbaceous plant, with long leaves rising from a woody root-stock. Each leaf has threads of its substance torn off at the margin, but persistent, holding on at the base. The colour of the leaf is a pale yellow, striped with two shades of green; the edges towards the base slightly tinged with pink.

Culture. This plant requires a well-drained sound loamy soil, with a little well-rotted cow-dung, and should be planted in the open border, as its beauty is spoiled if grown under the drip of trees or tall shrubs. A bed of it for a winter garden would be a striking object.

Propagation. When the plant attains a considerable size, it sends out side-offsets; these soon make roots for themselves, and may then be taken off close to the main stem, and planted in a shady border for a year, then planted in renewed soil in the place they are to remain permanently.

For the specimen illustrated my thanks are due to Mr. John Smith, Curator of the Royal Gardens, Kew.

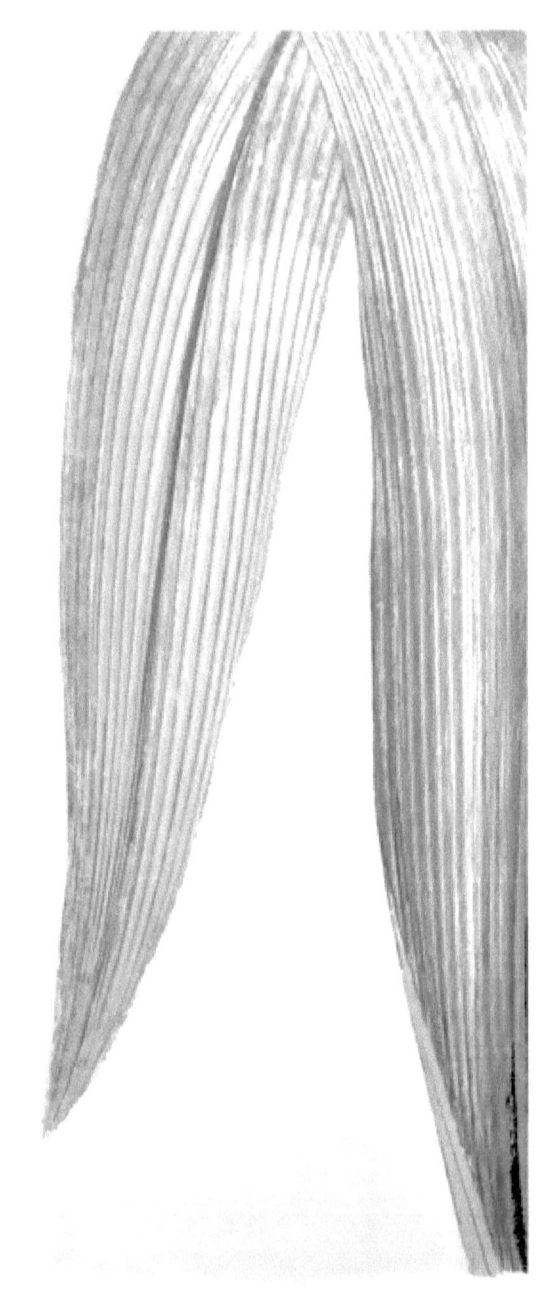

LII

CORDYLINE (DRACÆNA) INDIVISA.

UNDIVIDED CLUB PALM.

PLATE LII.

> "To the heart of a rose I told it;
> And the perfume, sweet and rare,
> Growing faint on the bright blue ether,
> Was lost in the balmy air."
>   A. A. P. (Cornhill Magazine.)

Cordyline, Club Palm, (from *Kordyle*—a club.) Natural order *Lilyworts*, *(Liliaceæ,)* Linnæus, 6.—*Hexandria*, 1.—*Monogynia*. Native country New Zealand.

Introduced by Messrs. J. and C. Lee, Nurserymen, Hammersmith, near London, in 1852.

Description. In its native country this plant attains the height of twenty feet. The stem is stout, erect, and undivided; on it the leaves grow in a regular and pleasing manner, attaining the length of five or six feet, and from six to nine inches in breadth. The colour is most remarkable—a rich bronzy green, the midrib being of a beautiful crimson brown colour, and having many red and white lines running parallel with it. The flowers are produced in a dense long spike, the side branches curving upwards; they are small, bell-shaped, and white in colour. This is a truly noble plant, suitable for a greenhouse or conservatory. As it is found at a high elevation above the sea, it may probably prove to be hardy enough to bear the open air in the south of England.

Culture. Soil, fresh fibry loam (from an upland pasture) two parts, leaf-mould one part, and sandy fibry peat one part, well mixed together with a liberal sprinkling of silver-sand, will form a compost in which this plant will grow well. Re-pot in March, taking care to drain well. Water moderately at first and through the winter, but plentifully when it is growing; and to keep the foliage bright, and clear from the red spider, use the syringe freely in summer. Place the plant out of doors from June to August in a sheltered place, where the winds cannot reach or tear the foliage. This plant belongs to the same genus as Yucca; treat it in a similar way, and it will grow as freely as that hardy tribe.

Propagation. This plant occasionally sends up suckers from the bottom of the stem; as soon as the base of the sucker has become firm, it may be taken off, potted, and placed under a hand-light, or a gentle bottom-heat, until roots are emitted; then give air freely, and inure to bear the full light and air, and treat it the same as the established plant. When a plant has grown tall, and consequently has a long stem, and a number of plants are required, cut off the top and treat it as described above for a sucker; then cut the stem into short lengths, and plant the cuttings overhead in well-drained pans, placing them on a gentle bottom-heat. The top bud, or perhaps two, will send out shoots, and afterwards roots, and then form nice young plants in considerable numbers, as there are eyes to every leaf.

The stock of this plant is in the possession of Messrs. Lee, and they inform me that they have all been raised from seed; they have but one plant that has attained any size shewing the true character.

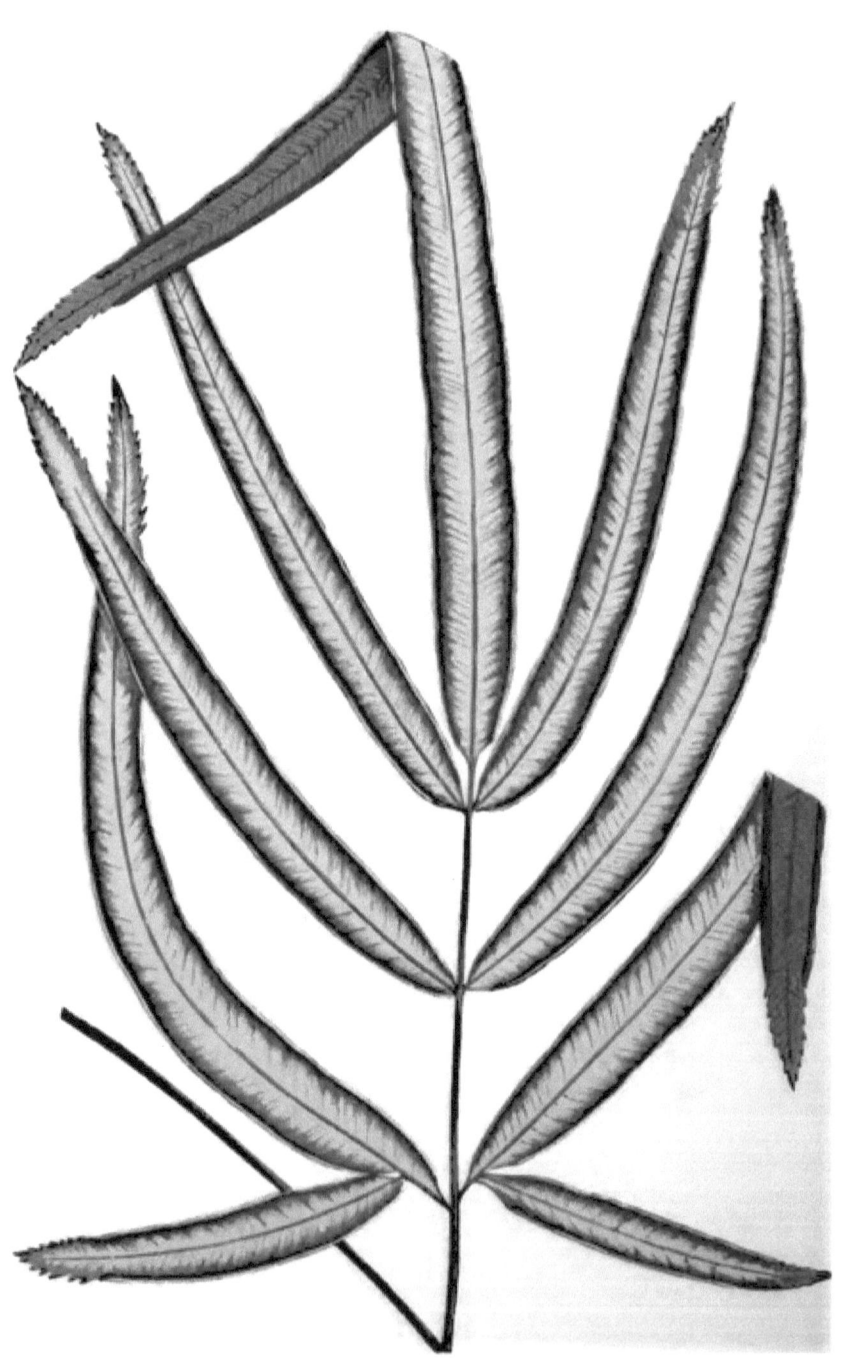

PTERIS CRETICA, Var. ALBO-LINEATA.

PLATE LIII.

> Away before me to sweet beds of flowers:
> Love-thoughts lie rich, when canopied with bowers.
> SHAKESPEARE.

For an account of this genus see *Pteris argyræa*, page 75.

Pteris cretica of Linnæus, Swartz, Willdenow, Hooker, Moore, and J. Smith, is known also as the *Pteris semiserrata* of Forskal, the *P. læta* of Wallich, *P. heterophyllus* of Poiret, *P. serraria* of Swartz and Willdenow, *P. pentaphylla* of Willdenow, *P. nervosa* of Thunberg, *P. vittata* of Bory, *P. multiaurita* of Agardh, and *P. triphylla* of Martens and Galleotti; the *P. stenophylla* of Hooker and Greville being also considered a variety of *P. cretica*.

This species is a native of various parts of India, including Calcutta, Nepal, Simla, Mussoorie, Punjaub, Boutan, and Sikkam-Himalaya, (at a height of six thousand feet above the sea.) Also of Java, Ceylon, Luzon, Sandwich Islands, Feejee Islands, Loochoo, Mexico, Guatemala, Persia, South Africa, Arabia, Abyssinia, Corsica, Crete, Nice, and Siberia— in the Caucasian provinces.

The present variegated variety has already obtained the synonyme of *bicolor* by some of the London Nurserymen.

It was sent to Kew in the variegated state by M. Bennendyk, of the Botanic Gardens, Buitenzorg, Java, in 1860.

Description. This is the handsomest of all the variegated Ferns yet introduced into England, and at the same time requires but little management in order to produce a handsome specimen. The colour is a milky white, shaded off into a deep green margin to the fronds. It succeeds well in a warm greenhouse.

After having been grown to a moderate-sized plant, *P. tricolor*, like its parent, *P. aspericaulis*, requires careful attention, and the fronds are very apt to turn brown if not kept in a close warm shady house. It is a plant that requires similar treatment to *Cissus discolor* and *Cyanophyllum magnificum*, and should never be syringed under any circumstances. It is a magnificent Fern, and easily grown; it attains a large size, yet bears only a few good fronds at the same time.

Pteris cretica, var. albo-lineata keeps very dwarf, and makes a neat bushy plant, not more than twelve inches above the pot. The original plant at the Royal Gardens, Kew, has three or four dozen fronds upon it at this time, and Mr. C. W. Crocker, who has the management of the Ferns, says that the fronds remain a very long time in perfection, in fact that it is scarcely ever requisite to cut off a bad frond. The sterile ones are smaller than the fertile ones, and the pinnæ are broader, although the general form of both kinds of fronds is about the same. The stipes of the sterile frond is from four to six inches long, the whole frond eight to twelve inches. The fertile ones are more erect, and the stipes longer, being from eight to ten inches, and the entire frond from fourteen to twenty inches in length. The fronds are pinnate, with (usually) three pairs of lanceolate sessile pinnæ and a terminal one, which is half as long again as the others; the longer pair of pinnæ are bifid, or producing on their lower side a secondary pinnule of about half their own length. The next pair are also sometimes (not always) auricled, that is, producing a lobe on their lower side, of about one third of their own length. The sterile fronds and sterile portion of the fertile ones are spinulose-serrate, that is, with small sharp-pointed teeth, which adds much to their beauty. The fronds are somewhat curious, but very handsome.

Mr. Crocker has raised some hundreds of plants from spores and every one of them is quite true, not a normal green frond to be seen amongst them.

Culture. Requires a warm greenhouse. Soil, two parts turfy peat, one part loam, leaf-mould, and a liberal sprinkling of silver-sand. In this compost the plant succeeds well.

For fronds my thanks are due to Mr. Smith, of the Royal Gardens, Kew.

DIOSCOREA DISCOLOR.
LIV

DIOSCOREA DISCOLOR.

TWO-COLOURED YAM.

PLATE LIV.

"Ah, there are some good things in life, that fall not away with the rest,
And, of all best things upon earth, I hold that a faithful friend is the best,
For woman, Will, is a thorny flower: it breaks, and we bleed and smart:
The blossom falls at the fairest, and the thorn runs into the heart.
And woman's love is a bitter fruit; and, however he bite it, or sip,
There's many a man has lived to curse the taste of that fruit on his lip.
But never was any man yet, as I ween, be he whosoever he may,
That has known what a true friend is, Will, and wish'd that knowledge away.

* * * * *

And just one failure more or less to a life that seems to be
(While I lie looking upon it, as a bird on the broken tree
She hovers about, ere making wing for a land of lovelier growth,
Brighter blossom, and purer air, somewhere far off in the south.)

* * * * *

Surely I knew, (who better?) the innermost secret of each
Bird, and beast, and flower. Failed I to give to them speech?
All the pale spirits of storm, that sail down streams of the wind,
Cleaving the thunder-cloud, with wild hair blowing behind;
All the soft seraphs that float in the light of the crimson eve,
When Hesper begins to glitter, and the heavy woodland to heave:
All the white nymphs of the water that dwell mid the lilies alone:
And the buskin'd maids for the love of whom the hoary oak trees groan;
They came to my call in the forest; they crept to my feet from the river;
They softly look'd out of the sky when I sung, and their wings beat with breathless endeavour.

* * * * *

Nature takes no notice of those that are coming or going.
To-morrow make ready my grave, Will. To-morrow new flowers will be blowing."

OWEN MEREDITH, (Cornhill Magazine.)

Dioscorea, Yam, (after P. Dioscorides, a Greek physician.) Natural order Yamworts, *(Dioscoreaceæ.)* Linnæus, 22.—*Diæcia*, 6.—*Hexandria*.

Native country South America.

Introduced about 1820, by whom not known.

Description. An interesting herbaceous stove climbing perennial, with handsome leaves variously coloured with several shades of green, and having a pale glaucous stripe on each side of the midrib; the under side of a purplish crimson. The plant is tuberous rooted, bearing inconspicuous green flowers. In summer the foliage is very handsome. It is well worthy of cultivation wherever there is a stove.

Culture. This plant delights in plenty of room, and a light, rich, sandy compost of fibry loam, sandy peat, and leaf-mould, with plenty of river or silver-sand mixed throughout the whole. It displays its many-hued foliage to greater advantage if trained round a balloon-shaped trellis. Re-pot just as the tubers begin to send forth their young shoots in the spring, and if they are placed on a tan-bed for a short time after being re-potted, the shoots will then grow rapidly, and make a good display of fine foliage during the ensuing summer. During the growing season give plenty of water, but as the shoots decay in the autumn, gradually reduce the quantity; in the winter keep the soil moderately dry.

Propagation. As this is a tuber-bearing plant, it is easily increased by division of the tubers at the time of potting in the spring, and treating them as the old plant.

The specimen for illustration was furnished by Mr. Cooling, of Derby.

MARANTA ALBA LINEATA.
LV

MARANTA ALBA-LINEATA.

PLATE LV.

> "Ours is a garden, green and fair,
> And bright with flowers, in June;
> And spicy shrubs waft odours there
> To the high harvest moon.
>
> The chesnut's solemn boughs disclose
> Their thousand blossoms well;
> And hither comes luxuriant rose,
> Her tale of love to tell."

This charming leaved plant was introduced into England from the tropics, in the year 1848, and is consequently a stove plant.

In general appearance this plant somewhat resembles the *Maranta vittata*, already described in this work, (see page 77, Plate XXXVIII.)

The leaves are a rich green, covered with conspicuous white stripes.

M. alba-lineata attains the height of twelve inches, and when well grown is an excellent exhibition plant.

It requires the same treatment as that for *M. regalis*.

My thanks are due to Messrs. Rollisson, of Tooting, and Messrs. Veitch, of Chelsea, for plants of this species.

(

TUSSILAGO FARFARA FOLIIS VARIEGATIS.

THE VARIEGATED-LEAVED COLT'S-FOOT.

PLATE LVI.

How happily, how happily the flowers die away!
Oh, could we but return to earth as easily as they!
Just live a life of sunshine, of innocence, and bloom,
Then drop without decrepitude, or pain, into the tomb!

The gay and glorious creatures! they neither "toil nor spin;"
Yet, lo! what goodly raiment they're all apparelled in;
No tears are on their beauty, but dewy gems more bright
Than ever brow of eastern queen endiadem'd with light.

The young rejoicing creatures! their pleasures never pall,
Nor lose in sweet contentment, because so free to all!
The dew, the showers, the sunshine, the balmy, blessed air,
Spend nothing of their freshness, though all may freely share.
Miss Bowles.

A HARDY herbaceous perennial. A native of Great Britain, growing in moist waste places, especially in a clayey soil. The name derived from *tussus*, a cough, because of its supposed property of allaying coughs. Natural order *Composites*, *(Asteracea,)* Linnæus 19.—*Syngenesia*, 2.—*Superflua*.

A yellow-flowering plant, blooming in March. The flower-stalks spring directly from the roots, and are covered with numerous narrow rays; the leaves, which do not make their appearance until the flowers have withered, are roundish heart-shaped, angular, and toothed, and are covered with cottony down or cobweb pubescence above, white and woolly beneath.

The thick cottony substance of the leaves, when impregnated with saltpetre, forms an excellent tinder.

The present variety is variegated green and white, some leaves being almost entirely white.

The roots are fibrous, with long fleshy and creeping underground stems, which, when divided from the plant, make fresh plants readily.

The specimen for illustration was kindly sent me by Mr. Cooling, Nurseryman, Derby.

HEDERA HELIX.

THE VARIEGATED-LEAVED IVIES.

PLATE LVII.

> 'T was a lovely thought to mark the hours,
> As they floated in light away,
> By the opening and the folding flowers
> That laugh to the summer's day.
>
> Oh! let us live, so that flower by flower,
> Shutting in turn, may leave
> A lingerer still for the sunset hour,
> A charm for the shaded eve.
>   MRS. HEMANS.

HEDERA, the name given to Ivy by Swartz, appears to be derived from the Celtic word *hedra* signifying *a cord*, in allusion to the stem of the Ivy.

Natural order Ivyworts, *(Araliaceæ,)* Linnæus, 5.—*Pentandria*, order 1.—*Monogynia*.

There are several kinds of Ivy, which are much esteemed for clothing buildings and trees, and for giving an air of antiquity to a place. They are also useful in shady situations in covering the ground with a green or variegated carpet, in localities where nothing else will grow.

The group of Ivies figured need not to be described further than by reference to the plate:—No. 1.—*Hedera latifolia maculata*. 2.—*H. Hibernica foliis-variegata*. 3.—*H. helix maculata*. 4.—*H. New silver edge*. 5.—*H. Gold stripe*. 6.—*H. elegantissima*. 7.—*H. Old silver edge*.

The above are all hardy evergreen climbers, except under extraordinary circumstances, as for instance, the intense cold of

Christmas, 1860, when 40° of frost played sad havoc amongst them. Even the common English Ivy became all but deciduous in this neighbourhood, as indeed also did the Common Holly.

Propagation by cuttings, on a north border in sandy soil, kept moist in autumn.

The Common Ivy, *(Hedera helix,)* will grow to the height of forty feet and upwards, and has sometimes a stem of great thickness. At Brockley Hall, Somersetshire, one has a stem twelve inches in diameter; at Morpeth another has a girth of one foot seven inches; at Gigean, near Monpellier, De Candolle describes one six feet in circumference at the base, covering seventy-two square yards, and being four hundred and thirty-three years old. Near Fountain's Abbey is an Ivy, the stem of which is two feet three inches in girth.

The Ivy varies considerably in its habit at different periods of its growth, as it does also in the shape of its leaves. When young it has a brittle, climbing, rooting stem, with alternate three or five-lobed leaves, which in winter, with its rich dark shading on a brilliant deep green leaf, adds greatly to the beauty of the plant. As the plant increases in size, the lobes of the leaves become wider, and the stem less brittle. Opposite the leaves are pushed forth tufts of fibrous roots, which must not be confused with the tufted fibres, by the aid of which the plant clings to its support; the latter are produced from all parts of the stem nearest to the wall, or other support to which it is clinging; and it is worthy of remark that if the branches are crawling on the ground, these fibres are invariably absent.

When Ivy has reached the summit of its support, it undergoes a change in habit, its climbing character ceases, and in lieu, erect branches of tufted foliage are produced devoid of roots or tendrils, and the form of the leaf is changed from the palmate to a lengthened oval shape; it then forms a bush two or three feet in height, surmounted by abundance of branches of interesting greenish flowers, each flower furnished with a separate stalk, consisting of five green petals, five stamens, and one pistil. The blooming time is October, and by Christmas ripe berries take the place of flowers. The flowers are much esteemed by many kinds of flies, wasps, bees, and some butterflies; and the berries supply food for blackbird, thrush, and wood-pigeon.

The Ivy is a tree of great repute amongst the ancients. Bacchus had his brows and spear decked with it; the people of Thrace adorned their armour with its leaves; the Grecian priests presented newly-married couples with an Ivy wreath; and in the mythology of the Greeks and Romans an Ivy crown was the highest prize awarded to a successful poet.

Ivy is at the present day used with Holly in the decoration of our churches at Christmas.

It is worthy of remark that Ivy does not grow wild either in America or Australia. In Asia Minor, about Smyrna, it is very common.

For the illustration my thanks are due to Messrs. Paul, Jun., Cheshunt.

ECHITES NUTANS.
LVIII

ECHITES NUTANS.

PLATE LVIII.

> She comes, she comes! and earth is shewing
>   A resurrection 'neath her eyes;
> Where her white foot is falling, glowing
>   Flowers from the dead, dark soil arise:
> Where her hand waves, the forest quickly
>   Puts on its cloak of leaves and bloom,
> And the wide heath, late dun and sickly,
>   Is gay with celandine and broom;
> And still, as glides fair Spring along,
> Heaven is all fragrance, earth all song.
>   NICHOLAS MICHELL, New Monthly Mag., April, 1861.

ALTHOUGH this plant has been in cultivation for more than a dozen years, and may now be obtained very cheaply from any of the leading Nurserymen, yet it is very seldom met with in our gardens, and still more rarely do we see well-grown specimens. *Echites nutans* is a plant, which, as our German friends would say, is "very grateful" for any attention bestowed upon it; in fact it is one of those plants, which, if properly cultivated, becomes a really charming object, but if neglected, on the contrary, it is almost as worthless as a weed. Under the treatment specified below, the leaves of this *Echites* are brightly-coloured, and as beautiful as those of the *Anœctochilus* family.

The name *Echites* is derived from *echis*, a viper, in allusion to the twining habit of the genus. It belongs to the natural order *Apocynaceœ*, and, according to the system of Linnæus, to *Pentandria*, *Monogynia*.

Description. *Echites nutans* is a milky-juiced climbing plant, with opposite lanceolate leaves, which are generally not more than three inches in length, and one in width. They are upon the young and healthy shoots, of a dark green colour, beautifully reticulated with a net-work of crimson veins. The plant very rarely produces its blossoms, in fact there is not an instance of its having flowered in this country. It is well worthy of cultivation on account of its foliage.

Culture. The only way to obtain good specimens is by potting several young plants together in a peaty soil, and plunging the pot under a hand-glass in a strong hot-bed, where the temperature is not less than 85°. The foliage should never be washed with the syringe, or in watering, but the atmosphere around must be kept as moist as possible. Under these circumstances the shoots will grow rapidly, and should be trained to a wire balloon-shaped trellis. Young plants should be raised every season, as if allowed to become old the leaves get large and coarse, are widely separated on the stem, are yellowish green in colour, losing their crimson veining.

Propagation. This is a most difficult plant to strike by cuttings; but if the thick fleshy roots be cut into pieces of an inch or two in length, these make plants freely, especially if placed on a strong bottom-heat.

The illustration is from a specimen sent by Mr. Veitch, of Chelsea.

CISSUS PORPHYROPHYLLUS.
LIX

CISSUS PORPHYROPHYLLUS.

PLATE LIX.

> The world has its flowers, 'midst troublesome weeds,
>   Looking up to the sun with delight;
>   Having sprung from the ground, from the smallest of seeds,
>   To drink the sweet dews of the night.
> L.

This fine climber was discovered in India by Mr. Thomas Lobb, the eminent traveller for Messrs. Veitch.

Description. A stove climber, with slender stems, rooting at the joints, and producing heart-shaped leaves, about five inches long, of a brilliant emerald green in the young stages of growth, changing as they become older to a rich purplish green. The leaves are convex, and being also longitudinally ribbed, with the rib depressed, the satiny richly-shaded surface is shewn to much advantage; the under surface is purple, and along the course of the veins on the upper surface are irregular, angular, livid, or pale pink fleaks or blotches. *Cissus porphyrophyllus*, although handsome, is not equal in beauty to *C. discolor*, and of much slower growth.

Culture. Soil, a combination of peat, loam, and leaf-mould in equal parts, will grow this plant well. It is a species that will strike very freely from cuttings of the young wood.

The specimen for illustration was kindly forwarded by Messrs. Veitch, of the Exotic Nurseries, Chelsea.

ALOCASIA METALLICA.

PLATE LX.

The earth being studded with choicest of flowers,
 Whose beauties are grand to behold,
Refresh'd by the sweetest, most genial of showers,
 Their charms one by one will unfold!
But the richest and brightest that nature gives birth,
Can never compare with THEE!—FLOWER of the earth.

The sky has its spangling of stars without number,
 That twinkle and shine in the night,
Till clouds draw a curtain, and bid them to slumber,
 Conceal'd from our wondering sight!
Yet the richest and brightest pass unheeded, for why?
They can never compare with THEE!—STAR of the sky.

The ocean has treasures of stars and of flowers,
 Whose beauties are hid from above,
Entwined in the gardens of waters, in bowers,
 The emblems of truth, and of love!
Yet the richest and brightest, whatever they be,
They can never compare with THEE!—PEARL of the sea.

The earth has its flower, and the sky has its star,
 The ocean its pearl, to admire,
But, oh, what are these gems, whether near or afar,
 To beauty that love doth inspire!
For the richest and brightest would fade and look sere,
Compared with the GEM that the heart holds so dear.

L.

THIS is one of the most beautiful and distinct plants which has been imported into this country for many years. It is a native of Borneo, and was discovered by Mr. Hugh Low, Jun., during an expedition to the Kina Baloo Mountain, and sent to Messrs. Low and Co., the well-known Nurserymen of Clapton, near London.

It is a member of the *Arum* family, *(Aroideæ,)* which produces so many plants remarkable for the size, form, or colouring of their foliage. According to the Linnæan arrangement it belongs to the class *Monœcia*, order *Monandria*.

Description. This beautiful *Alocasia* is a stemless plant, producing many peltate, fleshy, shining leaves, of a somewhat ovate form, from sixteen to twenty inches in length, and from twelve to sixteen inches in width. The leaves are of a purple colour on the under side, while the upper surface is of a metallic coppery-red lustre, which is very variable in tint, and, as it is very glossy, it reflects the light, and produces different shades of colour quite impossible to describe by the pen, or to reproduce by the pencil. Like the chameleon, this plant appears of a different colour according to the point of view from which it is seen,—red, blue, or purple tints follow each other upon the bronzy surface as the sunshine falls upon the plant, producing an effect which is perfectly gorgeous. The inflorescence is enclosed in a whitish spathe, which is tinted with a rosy blush, as are also the petioles, or stems supporting the leaves. This plant is perfectly unique in its beauty, for there is nothing in the whole vegetable world which can rival it.

Culture. The soil in which it succeeds best is a compost of very rough fibrous peat, mixed with a little well-decayed leaf-mould, and a plentiful supply of sharp silver-sand. The pots should be well drained, for, although this plant likes to be freely watered while it is growing rapidly, yet nothing is so injurious to it as water stagnating about the roots. While young it should be grown under a hand-glass, with the pot plunged in bottom-heat of about 83° or 85°. The atmosphere in which it is grown should be kept very moist, especially during spring and early summer. It must be shaded from direct sunshine.

Propagation. It is to be feared that there is no mode of increasing this glorious plant except by the slow process of parting; still, as it makes offsets very freely, we may hope to see it in general cultivation before very long. It is certain to command admiration wherever seen.

ADDENDA.

There are many beautiful foliaged plants that have not been described and figured in the present work, owing to its limited size. It is therefore desirable to give at least a brief notice of those that are worthy of cultivation, and although the present lists may in some respects be imperfect, nevertheless will be found exceedingly useful to those who take an interest in "Beautiful Leaved Plants."

"Consider the lilies of the field, how they grow; they toil not, neither do they spin; and yet I say unto you, that even Solomon in all his glory was not arrayed like one of these."

St. Matthew, Chap. vi, 28, 29.

HARDY AND HALF-HARDY PLANTS.

Achillia millefolium foliis-variegatum.—A very pretty, hardy, herbaceous plant, bearing a white flower.

Aconitum Napellis foliis-variegatus.—A tuberous-rooted, poisonous, hardy, herbaceous plant, with white flowers; growing three to four feet high.

Acorus gramineus variegatus.—A very pretty, herbaceous, grey-leaved plant from China, growing about eight inches high.

Ægopodium podagraria variegata.

Agapanthus umbellatus variegatus.—An interesting half-hardy plant, with blue flowers. From the Cape. Two feet high.

Agave Americana variegata.—A noble half-hardy Aloe from South America, throwing up a flower-spike to the height of ten to sixteen feet.

Ageratum cœlestinum foliis-variegatum.—A half-hardy annual, growing about one foot.

Agrimonia odorata variegata.—Hardy herbaceous plant, with yellow flowers.

Agrostis colorata variegata.

Agrostis vulgaris foliis-variegatus.

Ajuga rubra variegata.

Ajuga rubra fol. alba maculata.

Ajuga rubra fol. purpurescens.—Hardy perennials. About one foot.

Aira cæspitosa fol. variegata.—A variegated British grass.

Alyssum saxatile fol. var.—One of the prettiest evergreen garden shrubs in cultivation, bearing very sweet-scented white flowers, growing about one foot high.

Angelica sylvestris fol. var., (syn. *Apium sylvestris.*)—A water-side perennial plant.

Antirrhinum flore-pleno variegatum.—Hardy perennial, with flesh-coloured flowers, growing about one foot high.

Antirrhinum fol. var. aurea.

Apium graveolens, (Celery.)

Arabis alpina fol. var., (syn. *A. albida.*)

Arabis præcox.—A very pretty hard perennial trailer, bearing white flowers; well adapted for rockwork.

Arabis lucida fol. var., (syn. *Lepidium variegatum.*)

Arabis mollis fol. var.

Arabis procurrens.

Aristotelia Macqui-variegata.—A sub-evergreen tree, well suited for a poor dry soil. Ten to sixteen feet high.

Artemisia vulgaris variegata.

Artemisia vulgaris variegata aurea.—Hardy herbaceous perennials, growing about two feet high.

Arum Italicum fol. var.—Hardy herbaceous perennials.

Arum maculatum fol. var.

Arundo phragmitis. (The Ribbon Grass.)

Arundo Donax versicolor.—Should have a little protection during winter.

Arundo Mauritanica.

Asclepias vincitoxicum variegata.—A very pretty, North American, hardy, herbaceous plant.

Aspidistra lurida fol. var.—A hardy herbaceous perennial from

Japan, more curious than ornamental. Should be slightly protected in bad weather.

Astrantia minor fol. var.—Hardy herbaceous perennials from Switzerland.

Aucuba Japonica, (Spotted Laurel.)—A very handsome, hardy, ornamental shrub, used extensively for potting to stand in town windows and balconies; it is a plant that will do admirably in the smoke of London.

Ballota nigra.

Berberis vulgaris fol. var.

Barbarea vulgaris fol. var.—A natural hardy herbaceous plant.

Bellis perennis fol. var., (Belgian Daisies.)—This is a class of plant that deserves more general cultivation. There are a number of varieties, having different shades in the variegation. We are indebted to M. Van Houte, of Ghent, for the introduction of the variegated varieties.

Betonica officinalis fol. var.

Cacalia suaveolens fol. var.—A North American, hardy, herbaceous plant.

Calamagrostis arundinacea fol. var., (syn. *Phalaris elegantissima.*)

Calystegia sepium fol. var., (Variegated Bearbind.)—A very pretty, hardy, deciduous climbing plant.

Canna Indica, fol. var., (Indian Shot.)—Very pretty, half-hard.

Canna zebrina.—Herbaceous plants; much used in the neighbourhood of London, in flower gardens.

Carduus marianus fol. var., (Milk Thistle.)—A very handsome hardy garden species.

Carex Japonica fol. var., (syn. *C. muricata, C. riparia fol. var.*)

Centaurea candidissima, (syn. *C. argentea.*)—A half-hardy evergreen shrub. Canada.

Centaurea dealbata.—Hardy herbaceous plant, two feet high. Caucasus.

Centaurea gymnocarpa.—Half-hardy.

Centaurea nigra fol. var.

Centaurea ragusina.—Very pretty, half-hardy, evergreen shrub; yellow. Candia.

Chelidonium majus fol. var.—A deadly poisonous, hardy herbaceous plant.

Cheiranthus cheiri fol. var.—Half-hardy evergreen. Will stand a mild winter.

Chrysanthemum Indicum fol. var., (Conqueror.)

Chrysanthemum Indicum pompone variegatum.
Chrysanthemum Indicum, (Queen of England.)
Chrysanthemum leucanthum fol. var.
Cineraria maritima fol. argentea.—A very pretty plant, used extensively for edging flower-borders, and for ribbon-beds.
Cobæa scandens fol. variegata.—A very pretty, half-hardy, evergreen climber, from Mexico.
Colchicum autumnale fol. var., (the Variegated Common Meadow Apron.) Britain.
Comarum palustre fol. var.—Hardy herbaceous plant. Britain.
Comesperma variegata.—Half-hardy greenhouse evergreen, from Australia.
Convallaria majalis fol. var.
Convallaria majalis fol. alba-marginata.
Convallaria polygonatum fol. var., (Solomon's Seal.)
Convallaria Sieboldi fol. variegata, (syn. *C. angustifolia.*)—Hardy herbaceous perennials. Britain.
Convolvulus cneorum fol. argentinum.—Half-hardy.
Coronilla elegans fol. var.—Half-hardy.
Dactylis glomerata, fol. var.
Dahlia fol. var.—Half-hardy.
Duringea celesioides fol. var., (syn. *D. Amhursti.*)
Dianthus barbatus fol. var.
Dianthus Japonicus Heddewigi fol. var.
Dianthus plumarius fol. var.—Hardy herbaceous perennials.
Diplotaxis tenuifolia fol. var., (syn. *Brassica crucoides, Allysum dentatum.*)
Elymus arenarius glaucus.
Epilobium hirsutum fol. var.—Hardy herbaceous perennials. Britain.
Erythronium Dens canis rubrum.—Hardy herbs; very handsome.
Erythronium Dens canis albidum.—Early spring garden flowers.
Euphorbia dulcis fol. versicolor.
Euphorbia marginata.
Farfugium grande.—Half-hardy.
Festuca glauca.—A very fine edging plant.
Festuca variabilis.
Fragaria Chilensis fol. var.
Fragaria fol. var. aurea.
Fragaria fol. var. maculata.—A very handsome rock plant.
Fritillaria imperialis fol. var., (Crown Imperial.)—Persia.

ADDENDA.

Fuchsia corymbiflora fol. var.—Half-hardy.
Fuchsia globosa fol. var.—Half-hardy.
Fuchsia gracilis fol. var.—Half-hardy.
Fuchsia maculata.—Half-hardy.
Funkia alba-marginata.
Funkia cuculata fol. viride marginata.
Funkia Japonica cordata fol. var.
Funkia ovata fol. var.
Funkia undulata fol. var.—A magnificent class of plants, deserving more extensive cultivation.
Galeobdolon luteum fol. var.
Geranium macrorhizum fol. var.—Half-hardy.
Geranium pratensis fol. var.
Glechoma hederacea fol. var. alba lineata.
Glechoma hederacea fol. var. aurea maculata.
Glechoma hederacea fol. var. aurea marginata.
Glechoma hederacea fol. rubra.
Habrothamnus elegans fol. var.—Half-hardy.
Hedera Hibernica fol. aurea.
Hedera fol. argentea.
Hedera latifolia maculata.
Hedera helix maculata.
Hedera helix elegantissima, (tricolor.)
Hedera helix fol. aurea sulphurea.
Helianthus vulgaris fol. var.
Hesperis arabidefolia fol. var., (syn. *Limaria albiflora.*)
Heliotropium aucubæfolium.
Hemerocallis fulva var.—Hardy herbaceous plant.
Hieracum maculatum.
Hieracum pilosella fol. var.
Humulus lupulus fol. var. (The Hop.)—Hardy perennial climber. Britain.
Hydrangea fol. elegantissima.
Hydrangea fol. var. aurea.
Hydrangea Japonica fol. var.
Hydrangea Japonica fol. var. aurea superba.
Hydrangea Japonica fol. var. striata.—A very handsome class of hardy deciduous shrubs.
Hypericum humifusum fol. var.
Iberis fol. var.
Iris fœtidissima fol. var.

Iris marmorata fol. var.
Iris pseud-acorus fol. var.
Jasminum azoricum fol. var.—Half-hardy.
Juncus conglomeratus fol. var.
Kennedya bimaculata fol. var.—A very pretty climber.
Koniga fol. var.—Half-hardy.
Lamium album fol. var.
Lamium album fol. var. tricolor.
Lamium maculata fol. alba.
Lamium maculata fol. rubra.
Leontodon taraxacum fol. var.
Lilium candidum fol. var.
Lilium candidum fol. var. striata.
Linaria cymbalaria fol. var.—Well adapted for rockwork.
Luzula sylvestris fol. var.
Lychnis viscaria fol. var.
Mathiola tristis fol. var.
Melica cœrulea fol. var., (syn. *Aira cœrulea*.)
Melissa grandiflora fol. variegata, (syn. *M. secunda*.)
Melissa officinalis fol. var. (Balm.)
Mentha heterophylla fol. var.
Mentha piperita fol. var. (Mint.)
Mentha rotundifolia fol. var.
Mentha sylvestris fol. var.
Myoporum punctatum.—Half-hardy.
Myrtus communis fol. var.—Half-hardy.
Myrtus tenuifolia fol. var.—Half-hardy.
Nerium fol. var.—Half-hardy.
Neuroloma grandiflora fol. var., (syn. *Arabis grandiflora*.)
Œnothera maculata.
Orontium Japonicum fol. var.
Oxalis cornicata rubra.
Pastinaca sylvestris fol. var.
Petroselinum sativum fol. var. (Parsley.)
Phalaris arundinacea fol. var.
Phlox elegantissima fol. var.
Phlox sauveolens fol. var.
Plantago lanceolata fol. var.
Plantago major fol. maculata.
Plantago media fol. maculata.
Plantago monstrosa.—Curious.

Plantago corneformis.—Curious.
Plantago fol. rubescens.
Polemonium cæruleum fol. var.
Polygonatum multiflorum fol. var.
Potentilla anserina fol. var.
Prunella vulgaris fol. var.
Ranunculus repens fol. var.
Ribes grossularia fol. var.
Ribes nigra fol. var.
Ribes rubrum fol. var.
Rosmarinus officinalis fol. var.
Rubus corylifolius fol. var.
Rubus corylifolius fol. var. aurea.
Rudbeckia hirta fol. var., (syn. *Helianthus vulgaris.*)
Rudbeckia lacinata fol. var.
Rumia acetosa fol. var. (Sorrel.)
Rumia Sanguinea fol. var. (Dock.)
Ruta graveolens fol. var. (Rue.)
Salix caprea fol. var. tricolor.
Salvia angustifolia fol. var. (Sage.)
Salvia fulgens.—Half-hardy.
Salvia officinalis fol. var. (Sage.)
Salvia fol. var. tricolor. (Sage.)
Santolina rosmarinifolia. (Lavender cotton.)
Saponaria officinalis fol. var.
Saxifraga granulata fol. var.
Saxifraga sarmentosa.
Saxifraga umbrosa fol. var.
Scrophularia mellifera fol. var.
Sedum acre fol. var.
Sedum telephium fol. var.
Sedum telephium fol. var. atropurpureum.
Sempervivum arboreum fol. var.—Half-hardy.
Sempervivum arboreum rubrum.—Half-hardy.
Sempervivum Californicum.
Senecio Jacobæa fol. var.
Smilax fol. picta.
Solanum Dulcamara fol. var.
Solanum jasminioides fol. var.—Half-hardy.
Solanum spc Californica fol. var.—Half-hardy.
Solanum pseudo-capsicum fol. var.—Half-hardy.

Solidago ambigua fol. var.
Spiræa ulmarea fol. var.
Spiræa ulmarea fol. var. argentea.
Spiræa ulmarea fol. var. picta.
Stachys lanata fol. var., (syn. *S. Germanica.*)
Stachys sylvatica fol. var.
Symphytum officinale fol. var. alba superba in autumn.
Symphytum officinale fol. var. maculata.
Symphytum officinale fol. var. sulphurea.
Symphytum glomerata fol. var.
Tanacetum vulgaris fol. var.
Teucrium chamædrys fol. var.
Thymus serpyllum fol. var. aurea.
Trifolium repens fol. var.
Trifolium rubrum pictum. (Three-lobed Shamrock.)
Trifolium rubrum pictum. (Five-lobed Shamrock.)
Trilium sessile.
Tritoma Burchelli fol. var.
Tussilago farfara fol. var. (Colt's-foot.)
Urtica dioica fol. var.
Urtica dioica fol. var. nova.
Vaccinum vitis idæa fol. var.
Verbena defiance fol. var.
Verbena officinalis fol. var.
Veronica Andersonii fol. var.
Veronica Andersonii maculata.
Veronica chamædrys fol. var.
Veronica chamædrys fol. var. pulcherrima.
Veronica gentianoides fol. var.
Veronica spicata fol. var. (*V. corymbosa, V. maritima, V. stricta.*)
Veronica urtisæfolia fol. var.
Vinca major fol. elegantissima.
Vinca major fol. reticulata.
Vinca major fol. var. argentea.
Vinca major fol. var. aurea.
Viola odorata fol. var.
Vitis hederacea fol. var.
Weigelia amabilis fol. var.
Yucca aluifolia fol. var.
Yucca aluifolia fol. var. rubra.—Half-hardy.
Yucca filamentosa fol. var.—Half-hardy.

ADDENDA. 135

LIST OF DESIRABLE HARDY VARIEGATED PLANTS.

ORNAMENTAL BORDER PLANTS.
Agathæa cœlestis variegata.
Arabis lucida variegata.
Astrantia major variegata.
Bellis perennis variegata.
Epilobium hirsutum variegatum.
Iris Germanica variegata.
Lilium candidum variegatum.
Linaria cymbalaria variegata.
Melissa grandiflora variegata.
Mentha piperita variegata.
Œnothera glauca variegata.
Polemonium cœruleum variegatum.
Sedum acre variegata.
Spiræa ulmaria variegata.
Teucrium Chamædrys variegatum.
Tussilago Farfara fol. var.
Vinca herbacea variegata.
Vinca herbacea elegantissima.
Yucca filamentosa variegata.

VARIEGATED SHRUBS.
Aucuba Japonica.
Cupressus thyoides variegata.
Daphne cneorum variegatum.
Holly, (many varieties.)
Ivy, (Gold Variegated.)
Juniperus Virginiana variegata.
Mountain Ash, (New Weeping Var.)
Philadelphus coronarius fol. var.
Rhamnus alaternus aureis.
Rhododendron ponticum variegatum.
Symphoricarpus vulgaris fol. var.
Taxus baccata foliis argentis.
Taxus baccata foliis aureis.
Taxus baccata elegantissima.
Thuja orientalis argentea variegata.
Thuja occidentalis foliis variegata.
Thuja sinensis foliis argenteis var.

HARDY TREES.
Acer Pseudo platanus variegatum.
ÆsculusHippocastanum variegatum.
Castanea vesca variegata.
Quercus cerris variegata.
Quercus pedunculata marginata.
Quercus pedunculata variegata.
Tilia grandiflora aurea.
Ulmus glabra variegata.
Ulmus montana pendula.
Ulmus suberosa variegata.

EVERGREEN TREES AND SHRUBS.

Aristotelia Macqui foliis variegatis. Variegated.
   Aristotelia. A sub-evergreen tree, 10-15 feet.
Aucuba Japonica, (Spotted Laurel.) 6-10 feet.
   Japonica sub-maculata.

Buxus sempervirens argentea. From 6 to 10 feet.
   aurea. From 6 to 10 feet.
   glauca. "
   marginata. "
   variegata nova. Very handsome evergreens.

Cistus maculatus. Very pretty dwarf free flowering evergreen, 4-5 feet.
Daphne cneorum variegata. 1 foot.
    indica rubra variegata. 6 feet.
Ilex aquifolium albo marginatum. Decidedly the handsomest of all hardy ornamental evergreens; will thrive in almost any soil, but prefers a dry sand.
    albo pictum.
    aureo marginatum.
    aureo pictum.
    ciliatum.
    ferox aureum.
    recurvum variegatum. Loam, 10-15 feet.
Ilex laurifolium.
Laurus nobilis. The leaves highly aromatic.
Mahonia aquifolium.
Quercus agrifolia. 21 feet. Handsome evergreens of large size.
    heterophylla. 21 feet.
    ilex. "
    laurifolia. "
Rhamnus alaternus variegata. 10-20. Elegant evergreen shrubs.
    argenteis. 10.
    fol. maculatis. 10-20.
Yucca gloriosa. 3-5 feet. Handsome lawn plants.
    filamentosa. 1.
    flaccida. 1-2.

DECIDUOUS TREES AND SHRUBS.

Acer pseudo-platanus albo-variegatum. 30 to 50 feet.
    pseudo-platanus purpureum.
Æsculus Hippocastanum foliis aureis. 30-40 feet.
Alnus incana. 50-70.
Betula nigra pendula. 60-70.
Castanea vesca aspleniifolia.
    vesca variegata. 20-30.
Cornus mas fol. variegata. 10-15.
Cratægus oxycantha aurea fol. argentis.
Deutzia gracilis variegata. 1-2.
Elæagnus argentea. 10.
Fagus sylvatica foliis variegata. 20-30.
Fraxinus excelsior aurea pendula. 30.
Ligustrum variegatum. 6 feet.
Liriodendron tulipifera variegata. 20.
Philadelphus coronarius variegatus. 5.
Pyrus aucuparia pendula fol. aureis.
    communis fol. variegatis. 15.
    malus foliis variegatis. 15.
Quercus cerris variegata. 30.
    nigra. 15-20.
    pedunculata foliis variegatis.
Salix vitellina. 20-30.
Sambucus nigra fol. aureis. 20.
Spiræa argentea or nutans. 4-6.
Symphoricarpus vulgaris foliis variegatis.
Tilia Europæa aurea. 50-70.
Ulmus campestris foliis variegatis. 20-30.
    campestris viminalis variegata.
    montana glabra pendula variegata.

ADDENDA. 137

CONIFERS AND TAXIDS.

Abies excelsa variegata finedonensis. 50.
Cedrus libani foliis argenteis. 50-100.
Picea amabilis. 100.
Pinus sylvestris argentea. 10-50.
Chamæcyparis sphæroides variegata. 6-10.

Juniperus sabina foliis variegatis. 2-4.
  virginiana foliis aurea. 6-10.
Thuja aurea. 6-10.
  orientalis foliis variegatis.
Taxus baccata variegata. 6-10.
  fastigiata foliis aureis. 4-6.

STOVE AND GREENHOUSE PLANTS.

STOVE.
Alloplectus schlimi.
  speciosus.
Anœctochilus lowi.
  roxburghi.
  intermedius.
  cordatus.
  (spiranthes) eldorado.
  (macodes) petola, (a reseau dore.)
  striatus.
  (macodes) veitchi, (a reseau argente.)
  xanthophyllus.
  lobbi.
  pictus.
  argenteus (physiurus.)
  setaceus (aureus.)
Ananassa variegata pinangensis.
Aralia reticulata.
  leptophylla
Aristolochia leuconeura.
Begonia albo-plagiata.
  amabilis.
  arborescens.
  argentea.
  argentea splendens.
  grandis.
  griffithi.
  hederæfolia (nouveau.)

Begonia isis.
  lazuli.
  leopoldi.
  Madame Wagner.
  Madame Alwart.
  Medusæ.
  Medusæ d'Assam.
  nebulosa.
  Prince Troubetzkoi.
  Queen Victoria.
  rollissoni.
  richenheimi.
  rex.
  rex leopardi.
  ricinifolia maculata.
  roylei.
  rosacea.
  splendida.
  splendida argentea.
  thwaitesi.
  urania.
  victoria.
  virginia.
  marshalli.
Bertolonia maculata.
  marmorea.
Bignonia marmorata.
Bœhmeria argentea.
Caladium argyrites.

T

Caladium bicolor.
  bicolor splendens.
  chantini.
  houletti.
  balingii.
  marmoratum.
  metalicum.
  baraguinii.
  wrighti.
  picturatum.
Campylobotrys argyroneura.
  discolor.
Cissus discolor.
  porphyrophyllus.
Cassignya borbonica.
Croton cascarilla.
  discolor.
  angustifolium fol. pictis.
  pictum.
  variegatum.
Cyanophyllum magnificum.
  metallicum.
Dioscorea species.
  discolor.
Dracæna ferrea.
  ferrea versicolor, (terminalis.)
  nobilis.
  maculata.
  tesselata.
Heliconia aurea.
  metallica.
Maranta alba-lineata.
  rosea-lineata.
  arundinacea rubescens.
  fasciata.
  metallica.
  micans.
  pardina, (calathea.)
  porteana.
  pulchella.
  regalis.
  variegata.
  vittata.
  warczewiczi.
  zebrina.
  bicolor.
  eximia.

Maranta sanguinea.
Mikania speciosa.
Musa zebrina.
  cavendishi.
Podocarpus japonicus elegantissimus.
Pavetta borbonica.
Physurus querciticola.
Pothos argyrea.
Sansevicra guineensis.
Sonerila alba.
  margaritacea.
  superba.
Spigelia aenea.
Yucca quadricolor.
Nepenthes ampullacea.
  lævis.
  phyllamphora.
  rafflesiana.
  lowii.
  hookeri.
  distillatoria;
Cephalotus follicularis, (Australian Pitcher Plant.)
Dionæa muscipula,(Venus' Fly-trap.)
Aphelandra leopoldi.
  porteana.
Arum zebrinum.
Aspidistra elatior fol. vittatis.
Canna warczewiczi.
Dieffenbachia maculata.
Graptophyllum pictum.
Hæmadictyon nutans, (echites.)
Hibiscus variegata.
Hoya foliis variegatis.
  foliis picta.
Pandanus javanicus fol. var.
Plectranthus concolor picta.
Tillandsia splendens.
  zonata fol. brunneis.
  zonata fol. viridibus.
Ardisia crenulata, (ornamental fruit.)
  crenulata fructa-alba.
Billbergia vittata.
Cephalotus follicularis.
Coccocypselum discolor.
Cassignia borbonica.
Cupania filicifolia.

Dichorisandra vittata variegata.
Gesnera zebrina.
Goodyera discolor.
   pubescens.
Limonia fol. luteo var.
Mussænda frondosa.
Nerium splendens fol. variegata.
Rhopala corcovadensis.
   complicata.
   elegans.
   magnifica.
Vriesia splendens.
Ficus barbata.
   elasticus.

GREENHOUSE.

Azalia indica variegata.
Agathea variegata.
Agave americana variegata.
Ageratum fol. variegatum.
Aralia venusta.

Aralia capitata.
   macrophylla.
   palmata.
Brjaria tricolor.
Cineraria maritima.
Cobœa scandens variegata.
Daphne collina variegata.
Harbrothamnus elegans fol. var.
Hardenbergia monophylla fol. var.
Hydrangia japonica fol. albo-var.
Nerium splendens fol. var.
Primula sinensis glauca.
   sinensis, (fern-leaved.)
Salvia officinalis variegata.
Sempervivum arbor variegatum.
   tabulare.
Thea bohea.
   viridis.
Yucca aloifolia variegata.
   aloifolia picta.

ADDITIONAL STOVE AND GREENHOUSE PLANTS.

Adhatoda ænea.   Variegated stove plants.
   cydonæfolia.
Æchmea corallina.   Stove, ornamental foliage.
   fulgens.
   fulgens discolor.
   milinoni.
   miniata.
Afzelia discolor.   Stove, ornamental.
Aletris fragrans.   "
Anthurium amplum.   Ornamental leaves, stove.
   hookeri.
   macrophyllum.
   ochrantuum.
   podophyllum.
   rubronervum.

Aralia gracilis.   Ornamental stove.
   jatrophæfolia.
   lanigera.
   leptophylla.
   papyracea.   (Rice-paper plant.)
   parasitica.
   reticulata.
   longifolia.
   pulchra.
   sieboldti.
   farinifera.
   crassifolia.   Greenhouse.
   crassifolia integrifolia.
   quinquifolia.
   trifoliata.
   shefflerii.
Arum cornutum.   Variegated, stove.
   viviparum.

Arum marginatum.
Artanthe rollissonii. Ornamental stove.
Astrapœa wallichii. Ornamental stove.
Areca banksi. (Palm.) Stove.
   humilis.
   lutescens.
   rubra.
Artocarpus incisa. (Bread-fruit tree.) Stove.
   rigida-vera.
Astrocaryum mexicanum. (Palm.) Stove.
Attalea spectabilis. (Palm.) Stove.
Acacia argyrophylla. Ornamental, greenhouse.
   dealbata.
   lophantha.
Agapanthus umbellatus fol. variegatis. Variegated, greenhouse.
Agnostus integrifolius.
   sinuatus. (Stenocarpus cunninghamii.)
Araucaria bidwillii. Greenhouse, ornamental.
   cookii.
   cunninghamii.
   excelsa.
   excelsa glauca.
Arundo donax variegata. Greenhouse, variegated.
Aster argyrphyllus. Greenhouse.
Barringtonia racemosa. Ornamental stove.
Bischoffia javanica. Stove, ornamental.
Brassaiopsis speciosa. Stove, ornamental.
Brexia chrysophylla. Stove, ornamental.
   inermis.
   madagascariensis.
Brownea capitellata. Stove, ornamental.
   coccinea.
   erecta.
   grandiceps.

Beschonnera yuccoides. Stove.
Billbergia brayiana. Stove, ornamental.
   discolor.
   gigantea.
   granulosa.
   marmorata.
   morelliana.
   rhodocyanea.
   splendida.
   thyrsoidea.
Bonapartea juncea. Stove.
Bromelia spectrum.
Cereus triangularis pictus. Stove, variegated.
Cheirostemon platanoides. Stove, ornamental.
Chirita sinensis variegata. Stove.
Chrysophyllum macrophyllum. Stove. ferrugineum.
Cissus discolor. Stove, variegated climber.
Clusia flava. Ornamental, stove.
Colea commersonii. Stove.
Cycas tenuifolia. Ornamental stove.
   circinalis.
   revoluta.
   intermedia.
Chamærops excelsa. Greenhouse ornamental Palms.
   humilis.
   elegans.
   gracilis.
   humilis folius erectus.
   griffithiana.
   martiniana. Stove.
   palmetto. Stove.
Citus amantium foliis variegatus. Greenhouse.
Calamus micranthus. (Palm.) Stove.
   verus.
   viminalis.
Carludovica pumila. (Palm.) Stove.
   macropoda.
   palmœfolia.
Caryota urens. (Palm.)
Ceroxylon andicola. (Wax-palm.) Stove.

Ceroxylon ferruginea.
Chamædorea Ernesté-Augusta.
    (Palm.) Stove.
    casperiana.
    desmonicoides.
    oblongata.
Cocos comosa. Stove. (Palm.)
    denais.
    flexuosa.
    nucifera. (Cocoa-nut.)
Coleus blumei. Stove.
    pectinatus.
    thwaitesi.
Corypha australis. (Palm.) Stove.
    gebanga.
Dasylirion acrotriche. Stove, ornamental.
Dæmonorops asperrima. Stove.
    (Palm.)
    latispinus.
    melanochætes.
Dasylirion longifolium. Stove.
    texanum.
Dichorizandra vittata variegata.
Dion edule.
Duranta baumgardi.
Dacrydium cupressinum. Greenhouse.
    elatum.
    franklini.
    taxifolium.
Dammara australis. Greenhouse.
    bidwilli.
    browni.
    obtusa.
Dasilyrion serratifolium. Greenhouse.
Elæodendron longifolium. Stove.
    orientate.
Encephalartus caffra. Stove.
Eranthemum leuconervum. Variegated stove.
Erythrochiton brasiliensis. Stove.
    macrophyllum.
Exostemma macrophylla. Stove.
Encholirion jonghi. Stove.
Fagræa auriculata. Stove.

Ficus amazonica. Stove.
    indica.
    leopoldi.
    nymphæfolia.
    proscendens.
    repens.
    collina.
    diversifolia.
    falcata.
    lucida.
    macrophylla.
    panduræformis.
    religiosa.
Freycinetia baueri. Stove.
Fourcroya gigantea. Stove.
Gastonia palmata.
Guzmannia erythrolepis. Stove.
    picta.
    tricolor.
    spectabilis.
    pubescens.
Gustavia augusta. Stove.
Hippomane spinosa. Stove.
Inga brevipes. Stove.
    tweediana.
Jacaranda caroba. Stove.
    floribunda.
    mimosæfolia.
Jasminum gracile variegatum. Stove.
Jatropha multifida. Stove.
    panduræfolia.
Jonesia asoca. Stove.
Justicia zebrini. Stove.
Lematophyllum borbonicum. Stove.
Livistonia jenkinsoni. Stove.
    (Palm.)
Latania borbonica. Stove. (Palm.)
Licuala elegans. Stove. (Palm.)
Lomatia ferruginea. Greenhouse.
    bidwilli.
    elegantissima.
    polyantha.
    silaifolia.
Myrtus filicifolia. Greenhouse.
Mahonia leschenaulti. Greenhouse.
    nepalensis.
    japonica.

Mahonia intermedia.
　beali.
Magnolia fragrantissima.　Stove.
　ovata.
Metrodorea atropurpurea.　Stove.
Martinezia caryotæfolia.　Stove.
　(Palm.)
Neottia muculata.　Stove.
Nepenthes. (Pitcher Plants.) Stove.
　vittata.
　albo-marginata.
　distillatoria.
　lanata.
　sanguinea.
Nidularium fulgens.　Stove.
　pictum.
Niphæa rubida.　Stove.
Ouvirandra fenestralis.　Stove
　aquatic.
Oreopanax bonplandianum.　Stove.
　lanigerum.
　hypargyreum.
　peltatum.
　lindeni.
Orontia japonica.　Stove.
Phormium tenax.　Greenhouse.
Panax excelsa.　Stove.
Papyrus antiquorum.　Stove.
Pavetta caffra.　Stove.
　indica.
　owariensis.
Philodendron erubescens.　Stove.
　fenestratum.
　macrophyllum.
　microphyllum.
　pertusum.
　pinnatum.
　pinnatifidum.
Phœnix dactylifera. (Date Palm.)
　humilis.　Stove.
Pincinectitia tuberculata.　Stove.
　glauca.
Pitcairnia altensteini.　Stove.
　fruticosa.
　punicea.
Plectocomia elongata. (Palm.)
　Stove.

Phrynium trifasciatum.　Stove.
Phyllarthron comorense.　Stove.
Pilocarpus pinnatifidus.　Stove.
Pogonia discolor.
Psychotria leucantha.　Stove.
Puya altensteini.　Stove.
Quadria heterophylla.　Greenhouse.
Rhaphis flabelliformis. (Palm.)
　Stove.
Raphistemma pulchellum.
Sciadaphyllum pulchrum.　Stove.
　fariniferum.
Sindapsus pinnatus.　Stove.
Seaforthia elegans.　Stove. (Palm.)
　australis.
Smilax ceylonense.　Stove.
Stadmannia australis. (Cupania
　cunninghami.)　Stove.
　jonghei.
Stenorhynchus maculata.　Stove.
Strelitzia augusta.　Stove.
Sabal umbraculifera. (Palm.) Stove.
　blackburniana.
Sterculia palmata.　Stove.
　sps.　New Zealand.
Stenocarpus cunninghami.　Green-
　house.
Saguerus langkab.　Stove. (Palm.)
Saribus zollingeri.
Stachiophobe deckeriana.
Theophrasta jussieui.　Stove.
　glauca.
　macrophylla.
　imperialis.
　latifolia.
　longifolia.
　ornata.
　speciosa.
　warczewiczi.
Tradescantia argentea.　Stove.
　discolor lineata.
　odoratissima.
　zebrina.
　variegata.
Thrinax argentea. (Palm.)　Stove.
Trithrinax mauritiæformis. (Palm.)
　Stove.

ADDENDA. 143

Thibaudia javanica. Greenhouse.
Villarezia grandiflora. Stove.
Wallichia caryotoides. (Palm.) Stove.
Weinmannia pubescens. Greenhouse.
   tricosperma.
Xylophylla longifolia. Stove.
   arbuscula.
Yucca aloifolia var. Greenhouse.
   canaliculata erecta.

Yucca californica.
   filamentosa variegata.
   filifera.
   frankfortensis.
   stenophylla.
   undulata.
   variegata.
Zamia mexicana. Stove. (Palm.)
   picta.
   spiralis.

HANDSOME FOLIAGED FERNS.

Adiantum cuneatum. Stove Fern.
Allosorus crispus. British.
   concinnum. Stove.
   macrophyllum. Stove.
   trapeziforme. Stove.
Alsophila pruinata. Stove.
Asplenium dimorphum. Greenhouse.
   lucidum. Greenhouse.
   præmorsum. Greenhouse.
   serra. Greenhouse.
   viviparum. Stove.
   rachirhizon. Stove.
   trichomanes incisum. British.
   filix-fœmina apuæforme. British.
      corymbiferum.
      depauperatum.
      multifidum.
      plumosum.
      polycladon.
      acrocladon.
Blechnum spicant ramosum. British.
   spicant cristatum.
   spicant concinnum.
Cystopteris dickieana.
Cyathea dealbata. Stove.
Cheilanthes elegans. Stove.
   farinosa. Stove.
   dealbata. Stove.
   argentea. Stove.
Cyrtomium falcatum. Hardy.

Dicksonia antarctica. Greenhouse.
   arborea. Greenhouse.
Dennstædtia adiantoides. Stove.
Drynaria morbillosa. Stove.
   quercifolia. Stove.
Davallia polyantha. Stove.
   dissecta. Stove.
   tenuifolia. Stove.
   hispida. Greenhouse.
   immersa. Stove.
Eupodium kaulfussii. Stove.
Gleichenia hecistophylla. Stove.
   dicarpa.
   circinalis.
   semivestita.
   speluncæ.
   rupestris.
   flabellata.
   dichotoma.
Gymnogramma javanica. Stove.
   chrysophylla.
   l'herminieri.
   martensii.
   sulphurea.
   ochracea.
   pulchella.
   argyrophylla.
   tartarea.
   calomelanos.
   speciosa.

Gymnogramma lanata.
Goniophlebium scriptum. Stove.
　subauriculatum.
　verrucosum.
Hymenodium crinitum. Stove.
Hemidictyum marginatum. Stove.
Lastrea filix-mas cristata. British.
Litobrochia incisa. Stove.
Lomaria discolor. Stove.
　nuda. Stove.
Lycopodium dendroideum. Hardy Club Moss.
Marattia purpurascens. Stove.
Polypodium vulgare cambricum.
　vulgare cristatum. British.
　vulgare semilacerum.
　dryopteris. British.
　alpestre. British.
Polystichum angulare cristatum.
　angulare semipinnatum.
　angulare proliferum.
Onoclea sensibilis. Hardy.
Osmunda regalis. Hardy.
　claytoniana.
　cinnamomea.
　gracilis.
Nothochlæna trichomanoides. Stove.
　pulveracea.
　nivea.
　flavens.
　hookeri.
Nephrodium molle corymbiferum. Stove.
Nephrolepis davallioides. Stove.
Onychium auratum. Stove.
Oleandra neriiformis. Stove.
　articulata.
Platyloma flexuosa. Stove.
　ternifolia.
　calomelanos.
Polypodium plumula. Stove.
　effusum.
　musæfolium.
　billardieri.
　nigrescens.

Phlebodium aureum. Stove.
　sporadocarpum.
Pteris umbrosa. Greenhouse.
　scaberula.
　aspericaulis.
　tricolor.
　albo lineata
　argyrea.
Platycerium grande. Stove.
　alcicorne.
Polystichum falcinellum. Greenhouse.
Struthiopteris germanica. Hardy.
Selaginella martensii. Club-Moss.
　galeottii.
　africana.
　densa.
　denticulata.
　eryphropus.
　dichrous.
　willdenowii.
　lyalli.
　lepidophylla.
　cuspidata.
　atroviridis.
　lobbi.
Scolopendrium vulgare crispum.
　vulgare cristagalli.
　vulgare digitatum.
　vulgare endivifolium.
　vulgare irregulare.
　vulgare marginatum.
　vulgare multifidum.
　vulgare acrocladon.
　vulgare multifidum crispum.
　vulgare ramo-marginatum.
　vulgare ramosum majus.
　vulgare sagittato-cristatum.
　vulgare stansfieldii.
　vulgare submarginatum.
　vulgare submarginatum multifidum.
　vulgare suprasoriferum.
　vulgare variabile.

www.ingramcontent.com/pod-product-compliance
Lightning Source LLC
Chambersburg PA
CBHW031730230426
43669CB00007B/308